Acclaim for
GOOD TALK, DAD

"Delightful…it is lovely, loving, and a must read."
— *Star-Ledger*

"A witty memoir." — *Parade*

"Affectionate and raucous." — *Chicago Tribune*

"An entertaining mutual memoir." — *Tampa Bay Times*

"I loved this book. It's no surprise the Geists have such broad appeal. I want them to be my dad and brother."
—Jim Gaffigan, author of *New York Times* bestseller *Dad Is Fat*

"Bill and Willie are the wittiest duo I know. Their stories are hilarious. Reading this book made me feel like I grew up a Geist!"
—Andy Cohen, host of Bravo's *Watch What Happens: Live* and author of *New York Times* bestseller *Most Talkative*

Also by Bill Geist

Little League Confidential

Way Off the Road

The Big Five-Oh!

Fore! Play

Monster Trucks & Hair-In-A-Can: Who Says America Doesn't Make Anything Anymore?

City Slickers

The Zucchini Plague

Also by Willie Geist

American Freak Show

Loaded!: Become a Millionaire Overnight and Lose 20 Pounds in 2 Weeks, Or Your Money Back!

Good Talk, Dad

The Birds and the Bees... and other CONVERSATIONS we FORGOT to Have

Bill Geist and Willie Geist

GRAND CENTRAL
PUBLISHING

NEW YORK   BOSTON

Grand Central Publishing
Hachette Book Group
1290 Avenue of the Americas
New York, NY 10104

HachetteBookGroup.com

Printed in the United States of America

RRD-C

Originally published in hardcover by Hachette Book Group.
First trade edition: May 2015
10 9 8 7 6 5 4 3 2 1

Grand Central Publishing is a division of Hachette Book Group, Inc.
The Grand Central Publishing name and logo is a trademark of Hachette Book Group, Inc.

The Hachette Speakers Bureau provides a wide range of authors for speaking events. To find out more, go to www.hachettespeakersbureau.com or call (866) 376-6591.

The publisher is not responsible for websites (or their content) that are not owned by the publisher.

Library of Congress Cataloging-in-Publication Data

Geist, William.
    Good talk, dad : the birds and the bees…and other conversations we forgot to have / Bill Geist and Willie Geist. — First edition.
        pages cm
    ISBN 978-1-4555-4722-7 (hardback) — ISBN 978-1-4555-8202-0 (large print hardcover) — ISBN 978-1-4789-5306-7 (audiobook)   1. Fathers—Humor.
2. Fathers and sons—Humor.   I. Geist, Willie.   II. Title.
    PN6231.F37G45 2014
    818'.602—dc23
                                    2013047232
ISBN 978-1-4555-4721-0 (pbk.)

Bill dedicates this book to Jody Geist, without whom there would be no book, and no beloved Willie, Libby, Lucie, George, or Russell.

Willie dedicates this book to his mother, who picked up the slack on the big talks. To Christina, his partner in talks big and small since the sixth grade. And to Lucie and George, with whom he looks forward to not having the birds and the bees talk someday.

Contents

Good Talk, Dad

Introduction

WILLIE

I was baptized at the age of nineteen. A group of us awaiting the Holy Sacrament lined up in front of the altar at Westside Presbyterian Church that Sunday morning, looking out at the congregation. Well, *I* was lined up. The rest of them were sleeping like little angels in their mothers' arms. I lurked there, all six feet four inches and two hundred pounds of me, a college goon among the babes. How young and innocent they were. How old and hung over I was. The people in the pews would have been well within their rights to assume I was the oddly brooding father of one of the kids, or perhaps an area photographer hired to capture the moment. Nope, I was there to be baptized alongside them.

It wasn't as if I had just found faith as an adult. We'd been attending church for some time—I'd even sung in the choir as a boy. It's just that my parents panicked one day when they realized I'd been in the church all those years without ever having been officially initiated. Better late than never, they thought—but they weren't the ones towering over the pastor as he came by with the holy water. Couldn't we have done this in a private ceremony before the service, as they do with the technical awards at the Oscars? *In a ceremony earlier today, nineteen-year-old Willie Geist was given the sacrament of baptism.*

The pastor blessed the babies and dabbed holy water on their heads, welcoming them into the church. When he got to me at the end of the line, he asked that I bend down so he could reach me. I recall a smirk crossing his face. There was a smattering of laughter in the chapel. The real blessing that day was that the Presbyterian Church doesn't require full aquatic submersion. Can you imagine that scene? Would they have rolled out an aboveground pool for me? Or why not just make it a dunk tank and let my friends take turns to complete the public humiliation? At least my parents were happy that day. They got clear Christian consciences as I got grown-ass-man baptized.

That's kind of how we Geists do things. We perform life's rites of passage a little differently, and we get around to them in our own time. It works for us, and usually makes for good family comedy. As a young boy, for example, every time I threw a penny into the fountain at Paramus Park Mall in New Jersey, I wished for a trip to Disney World. My parents knew full well about my life's dream to meet Mickey, Goofy, and the gang in Orlando. After years of some nonsense about how dreams couldn't be bought, my dad finally caved and made mine come true. Unfortunately that day came when I was thirteen and in the seventh grade. I had long ago accepted the harsh truth that the fountain next to Foot Locker was where children's dreams went to die.

By the time we finally became royal guests inside the Magic Kingdom, my Disney years were well behind me, but we went anyway because that's what families do, right? They go to Disney. My sister, Libby, was eight, so the trip could be justified as making *her* dreams come true. Just to be clear, mine drowned in a mall fountain in New Jersey.

Ask my dad today about the "Character Breakfast" on that Disney vacation and he will laugh with perverse delight. For the "Character Breakfast" you board a steamboat to nowhere (an homage to Mickey's work in *Steamboat Willie*, one assumes) for a morning of all-you-can-eat buffet and more-than-you-can-take Disney all-stars. Children shrieked gleefully as a parade of Disney characters danced one by one up to our table, posing for Polaroids and generally spreading the magic. All I could think about was the poor bastards in those hot costumes, having to get hyped up for another "Character Breakfast." My Dad looked at tall, lanky, thirteen-year-old me in that sea of Disney—about the same size as Goofy by then—and started laughing. I joined right in. Not quite how I'd dreamed it all those years ago.

A dad is supposed to take his kid to Disney World. He's supposed to get his kid baptized. Mine did…eventually. A dad is supposed to send his kid to camp, to teach him how to fish, to grill, and to drive stick. Mine did…kind of. A dad is supposed to talk to his son about "the birds and the bees," the value of a dollar, and responsible drinking. My dad and I had most of those talks. Well, some of them. OK, we didn't have a single one of those father-son talks.

My dad grew up in the middle of the stoic Midwest in a time and place where you didn't sit down and talk about your feelings a whole lot. I'm guessing 1950s Champaign, Illinois, wasn't a lucrative place to be a shrink. I never heard the fatherly phrase, "Sit down, Willie. Your mother and I would like to talk to you…" My relationship with my dad always has been based on laughter. We tend to avoid the other stuff. Even when it's big stuff. But that's what this book is for. We're going back to cover our father-son bases retroactively. Better late than never, right? Kind of like baptizing your kid when he's nineteen years old.

Chapter 1

The Birds and the Bees… of Which We Dared Not Speak

BILL

S orry I never got around to having that talk with you about "the birds and the bees," Willie.

For openers, I didn't want you contradicting me. I worried that you knew more about this subject than I did. They'd begun teaching it in elementary school! And if the surveys were accurate, the practical field exercises began shortly thereafter.

Jody and Bill, June 27, 1970

Willie and Christina, May 24, 2003

On the other hand, how many fathers actually have the Talk? (I'd like to see a survey on that.) At what moment do you have it? At what age? Where? Should it involve an AV component?

I envisioned our Talk occurring naturally, maybe at a roughhewn picnic table in the woods with chipmunks scampering about, a pair of cooing lovebirds perched side by side on a tree branch and Bambi turning to look on. Very mellow, like a stool softener commercial. But we never went in the woods.

I'd heard of dads who just turned the whole thing over to their parish priests. But what do priests know? (Don't answer that!) And wouldn't it have felt awkward asking our local Catholic priest to provide you with sex education when we were Presbyterian?

And by the way, why "the birds and the bees"? There's the whole pollination thing with bees, I guess, what with your stamens and your pistils and all that. But birds? I've *never* seen robins screwing, have you? A little French-beaking, maybe...

Now you take dogs...a talk about "two dogs in the back-yard and the bees," now that might make sense. Or "the bunnies and the bees." I must have figured the Big Talk wasn't necessary after we took that family vacation drive through X-rated Lion Country. Where to begin? What to say? I didn't want to be overly juvenile: "You see, Son, when a man and a woman fall in love and get married some-times they sleep in the same bed and if it's a double or even queen-size they sometimes get too close and Dad's dipping sauce gets on Mom's Bloomin' Onion and they make a baby."

Nor did I want the Talk to be too advanced: "Now you may hear other kids on the playground—on the jungle gym or the big slide or wherever—refer to 'BDSM'...well, the *B* is for..."

Maybe I should be more direct: "You know that stork-delivering-the-baby story? It's bullshit."

My father never had the Talk with me. I would have hated that so much. We didn't do "talks." The closest thing to it was my mother's leaving an obtuse church pamphlet in my room when I was about fifteen (which was *plenty* early, as it turned out).

The pamphlet set forth the rules of sexual conduct. Sex was definitely restricted to a man and a woman. Only one each. Married. In a church. Intercourse was to be conducted in the missionary position, with the lights off. And not for fun! For family. If you could manage to avoid the act altogether, so much the better. (Hey, Mary and Joseph pulled it off.) Oh, and nothing with the suffix *-job* or *-style*. These rules were from GOD!

For the most part, kids learn about the birds and the bees from other kids. We did have a health class in school, where the subject was mentioned, along with all the other disgusting bodily functions. The teacher briefly mentioned the sex organs but never explained what they were for, exactly, and none of us had the intestines—large or small—to raise our hands and ask. All I knew was that, looking at the chart, boys had them and girls apparently did not.

Most of what I learned was from Mike, an eleven-year-old who lived next door and was just a bit older and wiser than the rest of the kids on our block. Mike told us that by peeking through the curtains he'd observed the pretty blonde high school girl who lived next door kissing her boyfriend. Mike said the guy was at the same time "rubbing" her.

"What do you mean?" I asked.

"You know, like you pet Frosty," Mike explained, referring to my family's cat.

"Where was he rubbing her?" Tucker asked.

"In her driveway," Mike said.

"No, I mean…"

"All over," Mike said. "Mainly on her sweater."

"Why?" I asked.

"They say it makes girls hot," Mike said.

"Like when you rub two sticks together?" asked Richard, indeed a Boy Scout (First Class).

"Or like an Indian burn?" Tucker asked.

"I don't think so," Mike said.

"So is that good?" I asked.

"Yeah. When girls get hot they want to do sex," Mike explained.

A period of silent reflection ensued. "Nonsense," I thought. It sounded implausible at best to those of us too young to have the sap rising. Troy Donahue never rubbed Sandra Dee's sweater in *A Summer Place*.

Mike's father, a Shakespeare professor, had ten thousand books in their house, among them one published in England that set forth everything known to the Western world about sex. Sadly, no photographs. Not even a drawing.

Mike's parents weren't home so he pulled out the hefty tome, sat on the bed, and began leafing through it. Nothing under *hot* or *rub*, but after a half hour he came up with germane text under the heading *Arousal.* And damned if it didn't confirm Mike's farfetched explanation!

Still, I remained dubious that somehow the same technique used for polishing my old man's Buick would make girls want sex.

In future sessions the boys-on-the-block salon tackled subjects like dry-humping, the johnny-rubber machine in the Texaco men's room, and so-called blue balls—none of which were even so much as mentioned in Mike's big book. We were on our own.

I assume you and your buddies, Willie, were having similar conversations. But you were discreet in all things and at some point I sensed that the time for our Talk had come and gone. And let's face it, you didn't want to have it any more than I did.

೧

P.S. I turned up some old notes I'd scrawled for our birds-and-bees talk, which would have gone something like this:

"OK. Birds usually fall in love in springtime. The boy birds start showing off for the girl birds, hoping the girls will pick them as their mates. (Just like male humans, who buy red convertibles, pump iron, buy Armani jackets, score touchdowns, join rock bands, etc.)

"The boy birds don their most colorful feathers. They sing their most complex songs, sometimes adding a little superfluous trilling and too much volume, like contestants on *Star Search.* They often make spectacular flights in death-defying air shows. Some even dance.

"When a female picks a male and they're ready to, say, couple…to produce baby birdies, many birds' reproductive organs swell to the point that all they have to do is touch each other to reproduce. (Keep this in mind.)

"Now bees, bees can have sex in midair! Remember when we saw those big military planes refueling in midair on TV? Like that.

"Boy bees are called drones, and they all want to screw the queen bee. She mates with a dozen or more of them and after they've screwed, the drones fall to the ground and die.

"Any questions?"

Willie Responds…Uncomfortably

Well, you've just made a compelling case for why we never had the Talk. You've also ruined my Outback Steakhouse experience forever—"Dad's dipping sauce gets on Mom's Bloomin' Onion"?! Jesus, our Talk would have been a disaster. Please don't ruin Red Lobster for me with a "garlic butter on Mom's shrimp scampi" analogy. Just stop.

I agree with you, Dad, that the potential damage done to the father-son relationship by a botched, awkward "talk" far outweighs the benefit of a young boy's having his old man teach him where babies come from. That's why God made health ed teachers. And by the way, even *they* don't want to have the Talk. When it comes time to explain the birds and the bees, the teacher pops in that *Miracle of Life* DVD, turns off the lights, and hides in the back of the room while middle schoolers giggle through the fertilization process. The lights come up, kids get a quick lesson on how to put a condom on a piece of farm-fresh produce, and they're sent out into the world. Done. Leave it to the professionals, I say. Same reason I don't change the oil in my car. It's not my area of expertise and it would only hurt the car in the long run.

I guess there was a part of me, though, expecting—not *wanting, expecting*—to have a talk at some point, no matter how brief or cryptic. Seemed like something fathers and sons did. But maybe it just happened that way in the movies. I was thinking we'd have a chat with a message like the one Laurence Fishburne's character "Furious" Styles delivered to his son Tre in the movie *Boyz n the Hood*:

FURIOUS: What do you know about sex?

TRE: I know a little bit.

FURIOUS: Oh yeah? What little bit is that?

TRE: I know, I take a girl, stick my thing in her, and nine months later a baby comes out.

FURIOUS: You think that's it?

TRE: Basically, yeah.

FURIOUS: Well, remember this: Any fool with a dick can make a baby, but only a real man can raise his children.

Aaaaand…scene. Concise, straightforward, and profane: everything a kid is looking for in the Talk with his pop. For the record, *Boyz n the Hood* remains among my top five movies in the history of American cinema. There was a time when I could recite every word of the screenplay from start to finish. If, God forbid, something had happened to you, Dad, I would have mourned appropriately, of course, and then petitioned Furious Styles to adopt me.

It's too late now, but if you and I had had the Talk all those years ago, with you as Furious and me as Tre, I imagine it would have gone something like this:

Int. night. Geist basement. Bill and Willie
on the couch watch a Yankee game.

BILL: What do you know about sex?
WILLIE: What?
BILL: Mattingly's swingin' a good bat, huh?
WILLIE: Yeah. Do we have any pretzels?
THE END

So, yes, the truth is, I didn't want that Talk any more than you did. What son would? Gross. Besides, there's something to be said for fumbling around in the dark during adolescent on-the-job training—it's part of the deal. You can't be Clooney right out of the gate. In fact, I learned everything I needed to know about sex from the love scenes in *Top Gun* (thank God Kelly McGillis invited Mav over to dinner that night) and *Risky Business* (although I never had a hooker over to the house while you and Mom were away for a week).

You see, kids, back in the day, we learned from movies that we lucked into seeing on HBO or Cinemax late at night. They weren't "on demand." We ran into them by chance. We also learned from nudie magazines. The kind with paper pages, that someone had to go buy somewhere.

There was not an app to satisfy your peculiar taste in porn. Do you have any idea how hard we had to work just to see a naked woman, for God's sake?

Dad, you had written something for *Playboy* in the mid-1980s, and you had a couple copies on a shelf in your office at home. Madonna was on the cover. A lady without her clothes! And then more ladies without their clothes inside! For me and Tom Manzi, it was like finding the Dead Sea Scrolls. Now that I think about it, I'm sure you hadn't written a damn thing for that issue. You just had a couple of *Playboy*s in your home office, ya old son of a bitch.

Today you don't even have to walk into a 7-Eleven to buy a pack of condoms anymore. A high school kid today misses out on that uneasy feeling of walking around for several minutes, getting a Gatorade and some Cool Ranch Doritos while he waits for the line to empty out so it's just him and the cashier when that Trojan transaction goes down. Now guys just click on Drugstore.com and have an unmarked box holding a year's supply shipped overnight (to a third party's home, of course, so as to avoid Mom's detection). Sex used to be so much more humiliating.

Growing up a couple of decades ahead of the Information Revolution, I was flying blind. The first pseudo-romantic interaction I can remember with a girl was a platonic elementary school kiss with Laurie, our next-door neighbor on Gateway Road. If memory serves me, it was in her room. No idea how I worked my way upstairs into a girl's room at that age, but rest assured it would be a long time until I pulled it off again. Laurie was a great girl but I suspect that first kiss had more to do with proximity than anything else.

A short commute through the garbage cans along the property line, and I was in. It was a one-time deal as I recall. A test drive for both of us, and we decided not to buy. Plus, who had time for fourth grade romance with all the WWF professional wrestling to be watched and reenacted in the yard? Love could wait. Hulk Hogan could not.

There was a romantic gap of a couple years until we moved across town in Ridgewood, New Jersey, to "the West Side." I was the new guy at George Washington Middle School. Now, either the girls at my elementary school back on the East Side were Quakers and I didn't realize it, or these West Side chicks had taken French kissing as part of their fifth grade curriculum. I was thrust into a sixth grade version of *Eyes Wide Shut.* Suddenly there were parties every weekend in big houses where people were spinning bottles and disappearing into closets in seven-minute increments. When you're eleven or twelve years old and you disappear into that closet, you're really making it up as you go. Like Heisman quarterback Johnny Manziel scrambling when a play breaks down—you just go on instinct and make something happen, and hope you don't fumble. Take what the defense gives you.

We paired off at these parties with girlfriends. *Girlfriends!* I was a couple of months removed from stealing girls' lunches and dunking them in the basketball hoop on the playground at Glen School and now I had to *speak* to them? *Court* them? *Kiss* them? This seems like a good time to issue a blanket apology to my sixth grade "girlfriend" Amanda. I realize now that spending six of our seven minutes in Heaven admiring the array of laundry detergents in the closet was perhaps not what you had in mind. You see,

Amanda, no one ever gave me the Talk (thanks for taking the fall for me on this one, Dad).

Middle school is the spring training of young teen sex. You're just getting to know your teammates and learning to play the game the right way. High school, of course, is when things really get serious—the big leagues. Hormones. Booze. Cheerleaders. Cars. My freshman year, I briefly dated a girl named Christina Sharkey. She was beautiful, and smart, and really fun. I wrote her name on the towel that hung from the waist of my football uniform. People needed to know she was with me. I wrote the first letters of her name too big in permanent black marker, so the letters got smaller as they traveled down the shredded strip of bath towel from my mom's collection of linens.

The towel was impressive, sure, but I was a tall, skinny freshman with zits who bore a striking resemblance to Anthony Michael Hall in *Sixteen Candles*. After a while I just couldn't compete with the older, cooler guys. They had BMWs. I had a BMX.

A couple of years later, though, when Christina and I were juniors and those other dudes were off starting over again in college, we reconnected. We'd been good friends since sixth grade and by the fall of that junior year in high school I was ready to make my move. A group of us were gathered for a party at my best friend Mark's house on November 7, 1991. If that date sounds familiar, it's the one when Magic Johnson announced he had HIV. We huddled and watched.

Mark's room was on the third floor of his parents' house and he had a window out to the roof. We used to hoist cases of beer from the ground outside up to that roof with an elaborate series of pulleys—this to bypass the staircase, where his mother and father would have shut down our trafficking operation. Mark's dad, one of the all-time great guys, but a tough guy, occasionally performed unannounced sweeps of the third floor, looking for beer and women to expel. When we heard his voice, the beer went out on the roof behind the chimney. The girls were hustled into a crawl space. Bob Kossick was the Ness to our Capone.

On the night of November 7, 1991, Christina and I found ourselves talking out on the roof. As the night wore on, even without a "birds and bees" talk in the back of my mind or any sexual know-how beyond what a sweaty, silhouetted Tom Cruise had taught me in *Top Gun*, I made my move. I leaned over and kissed Christina Sharkey. It was time. Now, it was difficult to go much further, you see, because we were surrounded by our delinquent friends smoking Parliaments and drinking the warm Bud Light from behind the chimney. Everything worked out fine down the road. I mean, we do have those two grandkids of yours, Dad, so you know *something* went right.

A dozen years after the roof, I married Christina Sharkey. Mark was the best man. It's a fairy-tale romance story, really: two hearts brought together by Magic Johnson, huddled on a bed of asphalt shingles, enjoying fine beer and cigarettes purchased illegally with a United States Marine Corps ID belonging to Mark's older brother. Just the way Christina had dreamed it would happen.

The point of my telling you all this, Dad, is that things turned out pretty damned well without the Talk that neither of us really wanted to have. Now let's never talk about sex again. How about them Yankees?

Chapter 2

Letters from Gang Camp

BILL

I was never a camper, Willie.
    Kids in my Midwestern, middle-class neighborhood didn't go to summer camps much, and when we did go, it was to a camp of the Vacation Bible School variety. I attended Boy Scout camp one summer and went home early, halfway through, on parents' visitation day. Another year I was enrolled in a day camp held in a public park that was operated, unbeknownst to us when we signed up, by a

Willie relaxes between gang fights at camp

college fencing coach. It was thrust and parry all day long, baby, with only a lunch break from the lunging: hot dogs, cooked outdoors, because after all this was camp. There was also that YMCA day camp, which I don't believe had activities, just the complimentary gray T-shirt with maroon lettering: INDIAN DAY CAMP. Possibly a little plastic bead stringing.

Not much camping on your mother's side either. She recalls Camp Kosciusko in Indiana, a church camp where she and her fellow campers hiked into the woods and prayed a lot ("Lord, take me home"). She recalls it now, curiously, as "very stressful and constipating." She spent time one summer at Camp Fannie Bailey Olcott by the shore of Half Moon Lake in Minnesota, a camp that her mother had loved when she went there as a child. Jody was homesick and has PTSD flashbacks to cryogenic early-morning swims.

Your sister went to Camp Bernie about an hour away and wrote a letter home that made it sound as if we'd mistakenly dropped her at a black site for enemy combatants.

Dear Mom and Dad. I've had an OK time. First I started crying cause I missed you and then I got in a fight with Amy and everyone was on her side. And I don't like any of their food and I can't get any sleep around here. Mom call me. I'm not allowed to use the telephone. Say hello to Peaches [our cat] *for me. Love, Libby*

To make up for that trauma, the following summer we sent her, with a friend, to a picturesque horseback riding camp in upstate New York. You know how they say all little girls love horses. Nope.

Her horse Telstar (named after the communications

satellite launched in 1962, probably around the birth date of the horse) had one foot in the glue factory. After Libby clicked and kicked her way through two weeks of camp with nary a trot or a canter, she threatened to eat Telstar if counselors didn't give her a new horse. She missed several meals swearing and crying as she tried to pull off her super-glued riding boots.

I wanted you, Willie, to go to a *real* camp, up north some-place. A camp with crisp fresh air, mildly scented by great stands of pine trees punctuated with white birch, aside a lake of cool, but ultimately refreshing, shimmering pure water, with sailboats and one old wooden Chris-Craft, loons and the occasional moose, and evening song-provoking camp-fires after the flag was lowered. A camp you might fall in love with, returning year after year, becoming a counselor and making friends for life. And maybe a girls' camp across the lake within covert nocturnal canoeing distance. Was that too much to ask? A camp where you could imbibe the won-ders of nature, where you would gain an appreciation for the great outdoors, and where lanyard-making was optional.

You wanted basketball camp, basketball camp, basketball camp, and attended several: at Holy Cross college; "Five Star" (in your dreams) in some rural area of Pennsylvania; at the University of Illinois, where you stayed with your grandmother; and at the University of North Carolina, where you received a complimentary photograph of you shaking hands with venerable Coach Dean Smith.

Early on you attended church day camp, which focused on religious crafts. We have a shot of you carrying a sign reading GOD IS GREAT. (Jihadists later stole your line.)

The popular camp that upscale kids in town attended

involved prayer sessions and coat-and-tie dinners. Your mom and I didn't think sport coats and ties had anything to do with summer camp. But if not there, where should you go? We didn't want a camp where you'd wear camo, eat wriggling reptiles, and crawl under live machine gun fire either.

We performed due diligence, venturing to a vast, befuddling camp expo at the yawning Jacob K. Javits Convention Center in New York, where hundreds of exhibitors hawked their outdoor experiences. There were far-flung camps (one in Finland, for example); camps that all but guaranteed your young offspring would make the Yankees, or become a better Presbyterian, rock star guitarist, Oscar-winning actor, flautist, linguist, financial planner, or computer programmer. But these all had kind of a trade school ring to them. There were ADHD camps, fat camps, and "adventure" camps geared toward the antisocial, drug-abusing, criminally insane youngster.

The whole thing was exhausting. We were about to give up and leave, when suddenly we spotted the booth for a camp we'll call Camp Carson in New Hampshire. The owner, Al, sealed the deal when he offered to present a private viewing of his Camp Carson slide show in our own home. One cold day in March, Al was at our front door, toting equipment. He set up a projector and screen in our living room, fired it up, and—whoosh!—we were swept away to the verdant hills and glistening clear lakes of New Hampshire, where smiling boys of impeccable character and dental care swam, skied, and dined on steaks and ice cream.

We whipped out the checkbook. And in July, when we dropped you off, we felt really good inside, having put the extra effort into finding a great camp that was perfect for you. Oh, how we anxiously awaited your letters.

Willie's Version of the Story

You're right, Dad: Al put on a hell of a show in our living room that day. It's just that he left out a few details that, in hindsight, were central to the Camp Carson experience.

In our modern age of Yelp, where you can find a hundred reviews of anything on earth, from frozen yogurt to, you know, camps, it's easy to forget that we used to take things on faith. We'd walk in blind, for example, to try out a new restaurant in town without first reading online that there were rats scurrying across the dining room on one reviewer's visit or that another picked up hints of Alpo in the lasagna. We learned these things on our own, perhaps telling a neighbor over the fence the next day to "avoid the new Italian place." We had no Facebook friends to rant to, or Twitter followers awaiting our snark (@WillieGeist: "Exciting dinner at Dino's tonight with wife, kids...and THIS RAT! pic.twitter .com/HGA565 #PullUpAChairBigGuy #HealthCodeFail).

So in 1988, when a cheery guy in a pair of cargo pants showed up at your front door with a slide projector and turned his Kodak carousel through a collection of quintessential camp photos—smiling kids in matching T-shirts canoeing across a pristine New Hampshire lake, starting fires with only flint and birch bark, learning the value of a day's work while cleaning up the mess hall together, engaging in a little unsanctioned water fighting ("Hey! Knock it off, you guys!"), and generally overcoming their suburban neuroses while becoming one with nature—you bought in.

In your defense, Dad, the technology simply wasn't available for you to know any better. Sure, you might have chosen those other fancy, time-tested camps with glittering reputations built on generations' worth of tradition, where all my friends went with their blue blazers and their loafers, but I respect your willingness to buck convention and roll the dice on Camp Carson. Those places weren't us. I'm not saying it turned out to be the right call. I'm just saying I know where you were coming from. Plus, I suspect you got a nicer deal on Carson than those parents did on the blazer-and-khakis country club operations.

As you know, I wasn't terribly thrilled about going off to camp in the sticks of New Hampshire. I was a thirteen-year-old dude from the suburbs of New York City about to enter the eighth grade. There were girls to be chased at the Jersey Shore, endless summer basketball games to be played, and Yankee games to be watched. There was no TV at Camp Carson, for God's sake. The new N.W.A. album would come out that August, while I was making puppets on tongue depressors or some such nonsense. Luckily I negotiated you and Mom down to the four-week version of the camp, which was like having the little summer camp sampler platter and getting the check. Some kids stayed for two months. How much do you have to hate your kid to send him to camp for two months? I think I used that spin on you to some effect.

The other bit of good news was that we were able to dupe one—and only one—of my good middle school buddies to join me on this venture into the unknown. Matt Capell probably should have been at upmarket Camp Dudley with the rest of our crew, but for reasons I can't recall he signed up with me as part of a two-man package deal. Matt and I were there only to help our moms and dads check a parenting box. We were doing them a solid. Get in, get out—like SEAL Team Six. We'd do a little water-skiing, some marshmallow roasting, a little leaf identifying—or whatever people did at camp—and get back to civilization. So off we went to serve our time at Camp Carson. Little did we know.

Dad, if your goal was for me to grow up, well, you got your money's worth. But not in the ways Al showed you in that slide show. Matt and I arrived at Camp Carson in that summer of '88 as boys. We left as young men whose souls had been darkened by four weeks in the joint along Lake Winnipesaukee. We were like Tim Robbins and Morgan Freeman in *The Shawshank Redemption*, getting each other through the days by dreaming about the lives that awaited us on the outside. And believe me, we thought about digging our way out of Carson, just like Andy Dufresne did behind that Rita Hayworth poster at Shawshank (for what it's worth, our poster would have been of Debbie Gibson). You think I'm being dramatic with this prison comparison. Oh no, I mean it quite literally. It's true what they say: Summer camp changes a man.

There was a buzz one morning in the chow hall during the second week of camp. Some of us campers who'd come from all corners of the Northeast were sitting at a table getting to know one another over a breakfast of bacon, "bug juice," and black market Snickers bars when the volume and animation of the conversation at the counselors' table began to rise. There was a story. It was at that moment, Dad, that your romantic vision of summer camp shattered into a million pieces, and the distinction between Camp Carson and the-fancy-one-with-the-blazers-and-the-loafers was made as crystal clear as the water in that lake outside.

The counselors were getting into a heated exchange about something or other that happened after our "lights-out" the previous night. Not the fun kind of pranksters' exchange you hear about at summer camps, where one guy fills another's sleeping bag with shaving cream, he responds by putting Preparation H in the toothpaste tube, and good-natured, WASP-y hijinks ensue. No, this here was a gang fight, plain and simple, carried from the streets of the South Bronx to the woods of New Hampshire.

Turns out one of the members of the warring counselor factions had delivered on a threat by going out to the parking lot and slashing the tires on another gentleman's car as he slept. Presumably with that nifty bowie knife we'd used to fashion walking sticks for a nature hike earlier in the afternoon. Yes, our counselors were slashing each other's tires. I think you'd agree that stretches the definition of "prank" considerably.

There was talk that next morning in the chow hall of reprisal. There we were up in God's country, campers breathing the fresh summer air, and deciding over breakfast whether we were safer backing the Latin Kings or the Spanish Gangster Disciples. The stakes certainly had been raised for that day's game of capture the flag.

It was that same day that I learned what cheery old Al hadn't shared with you and Mom that day in our living room. Camp Carson served not just as a place for carefree boys to spend a magical summer but also as a safe, wooded refuge for convicted nonviolent gang offenders to serve out their sentences as camp counselors. Nice enough guys, most of 'em, and a noble experiment by Carson, but it just seems like the kind of thing that should appear somewhere in the brochure. Maybe a quick mention from Al after the slide show and Q and A? I know you didn't want us to go to some camp where we would be pampered and coddled, but I believe you had a right to know that "gang warfare" was on the list of scheduled activities.

When the counselors weren't fighting, they were loving... female members of the Carson staff. In the third week of camp, we were playing flag football and one of the campers tore up his leg pretty good. A group of us, including our counselor/notorious gang member, took the kid over to the Pillbox to have it looked at by the nurse, who frankly didn't see a lot of action up there at Carson. Mostly poison ivy and bug bites, I'm guessing. We tugged at the door of the small building where the nurse saw patients, but it was locked. Our counselor/Latin King knocked on the door. No answer. Another knock. Harder this time. Nothing. The camper's leg was bleeding and he needed to clean it up at the very least.

Then a sound from inside the Pillbox. Thank goodness, the nurse was in after all. Must have been in the back running inventory or reading up on the latest medical research. We knocked again. Still nothing, though. A few calls for her to open the door. Finally, after several minutes, the nurse swung the door open looking as if she'd just finished a triathlon...or a wrestling match. In a way, she had.

Short of breath, hair all over the place, clothes trying and failing to pull themselves back together. As she welcomed the young, battered patient into her office, a different counselor passed silently, head down, through the door on his way out. One wonders just how much blood my young teammate lost in the time it took for her to render her "private medical service" for that counselor. If memory serves, the kid lived, which is good. Knowing now what I know about their rivalry, I assume the counselors had been fighting, perhaps even wagering, over who would get to the nurse first. Well, it was *that* guy. In the Pillbox. In broad daylight. With a kid bleeding outside. Score one for the Disciples!

As my four weeks at Carson came to a close, there was a breakout of impetigo. I remember it vividly because, twenty-six years later, I still have a nickel-size scar on my forearm where the bacterial infection struck. The lingering effect may be the result of the care I received from the gang, if you'll forgive the term, up there. Impetigo is a pretty serious deal and it was spreading through camp like wildfire, so the horny, negligent nurse and the staff of gang members had to move quickly. Together they came up with a solution that fit the Camp Carson quasi-prison experience perfectly.

They told all of us thirteen-year-olds to strip naked and stand against a wall outside one of the cabins. We did. They threw us bars of soap, and told us to lather up. Then they dragged out a high-powered hose that could have extinguished an Arizona brush fire and sprayed us down as we fought to stay upright against the force of the water. I'm guessing the "nude power-washing" technique used to greet new inmates at federal lockups wasn't the impetigo treatment recommended at the time by the *New England Journal of Medicine*, but in our summer at the-camp-that-turned-out-to-be-a-halfway-house-for-convicted-gang-members, we wouldn't have had it any other way.

Knife fights in parking lots are so much more fun than prayer breakfasts in blue blazers.

Geist Date in History

July 17, 1979

Combining 1970s lax child safety standards with his own disdain for neofascist/crypto–New World Order mandatory seat belt laws, Bill Geist travels the streets of Evanston, Illinois, with four-year-old Willie jumping on the passenger seat of their Volkswagen Bug. Bill hits the brakes. Willie hits the windshield. They brush it off and proceed with their grocery shopping trip to Dominick's. Mom doesn't need to know about this, Bill tells his young son. Jody Geist learns about it in a book written thirty-five years later.

Willie gets into the front passenger seat in the days before seat belts or car seats

Chapter 3

The Red Jeep

BILL

My first book advance was ten thousand dollars, which seemed like a windfall. We posted a "$10,000 Jackpot!" list on the refrigerator door where family members could scrawl ideas on how best to blow the money.

The red Jeep, carrying
a normal load

Willie's
turn

Bill trolls
for a topless
beach

Suggestions were along the lines of "Box at Yankee Stadium" and "Private jet."

In the end we decided on "Red Jeep." At the time we were driving a company car, a bland beige Chevy Citation (aka "the Ci"), which was free, but caused us to don disguises when driving anywhere within a ten-mile radius of home. It was the kind of nondescript car driven by Sanitation Department administrative personnel.

We wanted something fun and different, although you kids were almost embarrassed to be seen in the Jeep since they weren't cool yet. My impulse to be fun and different has caused a lot of embarrassment through the years. Just ask your mother and your sister.

One rarely spotted a Jeep on the road in 1984 when we bought ours. Your mother and I are among the very first baby boomers and we always feel we're showing the way for the 76 million who follow. A year after our purchase I saw a full-page magazine ad showing a red Jeep driving along a beach, and the rest is history. Suddenly Jeeps and their imitators were everywhere, suburbanites using their four-wheel-drive off-road vehicles with all-terrain tires and hefty rhino-resistant bars on the front to go through the drive-thru lane at McDonald's.

The sticker price on the Jeep CJ-7 was about $7,700, as I recall, complete with a driver's seat, four-wheel drive, and four-speed (if you included reverse) manual transmission. We opted for the luxury package—"Oh, what the hell, honey!"—which added doors on *both* sides, a passenger seat, a back bench for two close friends, and a radio. The salesman said power steering wasn't really necessary—no worse than powerlifting at Gold's Gym, really—and it did seem a bit wussy for the vehicle that won WWII. I forgot to ask about shocks.

Right off the bat, we were unfazed by crippling snow-storms because we had one of the few vehicles that could plow through it all. Alas, the gray Volvo wagons driven by the majority of our neighbors could not.

Summer brought the Jeep's first big fling, a vacation trip to an island camp off Desbarats, Ontario, in the North Channel of Lake Huron. We had to pack tight. There was just enough room to shimmy two medium-size suitcases on edge behind the backseat. We crammed jackets and sweaters atop them until the soft top bulged. We slid tennis rackets and extra shoes under the backseat. Every niche was filled when we put the Jeep into gear and headed north, first to Niagara Falls, then to Toronto and points west. We were definitely the coolest people on the road.

You'll recall that the next year we went to Nantucket. The packing was about the same, with the addition of two bikes secured to the front of the Jeep and two bikes precariously unsecured on the rear spare tire by some ingenious device that had been designed specifically for that purpose but didn't work. (I may have picked up a raccoon trap at the store by mistake.)

As we made our way, those rear bikes shifted restlessly, seeming reluctant to go on vacation with us. One turned completely nose-down several times. Anxious, I constantly checked the rearview mirror, convinced the bikes would fly off, causing cars behind us to swerve off the road. I pictured courtrooms filled with ravenous personal injury lawyers and prosecutors bringing criminal negligence charges. "I was in a hurry, Your Honor...I wasn't familiar with what a raccoon trap looked like..."

I stopped several times to readjust the bikes.

We felt like real Nantucketers when we pulled off the ferry in the perfect beach car. We unpacked the Jeep, then hastily removed the doors and top, flipped down the windshield, and put her into four-wheel drive—not easy since we had to get out of the car and turn reluctant knobs on the front tires.

Beach driving was allowed then, before piping plovers started running things. (Would we really miss them that much?) We flew up and down the sand on thrill rides, we leaving our seats, the vehicle leaving the beach, launched by dunes. One evening we had twelve relatives piled in and on the Jeep, one sitting on the spare tire, as we bumped over seven miles of beach to Great Point for surf casting and a fresh-caught fish–free picnic. My three-year-old nephew yelled "No-doors-on!" all the way.

Do you remember the time just you and I were driving on Madaket Beach when we came upon a flock of topless young women sunbathing? I stopped the car. "Something wrong with the engine," I said, loudly, then sat back to contemplate the situation. "Could be the crankcase..." Your look of concern gave way to snickering as you looked around. I finally managed to get her started and we drove off, slowly. You were about ten years old. I suppose another father might have handled this more maturely.

Back then the height of automotive status in Nantucket was a funky, rusty, dented old four-wheel-drive beach vehicle, and after several vacations on the island, our Jeep was getting there. Its headlights went out one dark, moonless night on a trip back from Great Point. I had to drive the better part of seven miles at the water's edge to keep my bearings. Yep, ol' Red was definitely getting there.

But its work was *far from over.*

Willie Inherits the Red Jeep

First of all, Dad, I love your instinct to take that ten-thousand-dollar book check and spend every nickel of it as fast as you could, like a rapper who just got his first record deal. And like a free-spending rapper, you went for all the extras: seats, AM/FM radio, windshield—the works.

That red Jeep was part of the family, and a perfect symbol for us. It was loud, it was quirky, it was a little bumpy sometimes, but man, it always was fun as hell. Of course I remember those trips north with our bicycles dangling off the back. I had absolutely no expectation that my bike would be on the car when we arrived at our destination. We were resigned to the fact that there'd be a couple casualties along the way. But unless I've buried some trauma, we never lost one, never caused a pileup on I-95, and never appeared in court to answer charges. It seems there was probably a better model of bike rack to fit our particular car, but where's the fun in having the right model?

Now that you mention our "mistaken" trip to the nude beach on Nantucket—the one where you popped the hood and just stood in front of the car for several minutes not remotely looking at the engine—maybe *that* was our "birds and bees" conversation. You were telling me implicitly, "Son, you're gonna like those boobs down there one of these days." Sorry I missed the point.

If you and Mom had the red Jeep in its young, vital years, I took her through middle age, when she started to sag a bit. On May 3, 1992—my seventeenth birthday—the state of New Jersey saw fit to give me a driver's license. I backed over a few cones on the parallel parking portion of the exam, but the mistake was not fatal. That birthday was the same day I inherited the Jeep.

Remember, this hadn't been some vanity beach car since we bought it in 1984. It was our family car. It had gone to school every day, and to basketball practice and tap dancing, and to the grocery store, and on long road trips. The Jeep hadn't been sitting under a cover in a three-car garage waiting to be driven around the Hamptons eight weekends a year. What I'm saying is, she was good and beat up by the time she made it to me.

As a gift, you and Mom put in a new radio, with cassette player, and a nice speaker system. With no roof and no doors on the Jeep, I blasted Naughty by Nature as I whipped through the streets of Ridgewood. Now, in addition to no roof or doors, the Jeep often had no first gear. The gearbox had become bitter and stubborn over the years, so I usually had to punch the gas to get it going in second. And if I found myself starting on a hill, well, I might as well just roll back to the bottom in neutral and explore a different route.

Mom, as you know, taught me how to drive the Jeep

in the years before I got my license. Come to think of it, that's another one of those things I think you were supposed to do—at least that's the way it happens in the car commercials. (*Dad chokes back tears as he watches his son drive off to the junior prom in the car his old man taught him to drive. Where do the years go?*) Mom was a great and patient teacher. Teaching someone to drive on a manual Jeep CJ-7 with no power steering is like teaching a kid to read on Tolstoy. (*Sound it out, sweetie, "Andrei...Nikolayevich...Bolkonsky." No, try it again.*)

As Mom tells it, she would brace herself in the passenger seat and grab the metal handle above the glove box while I bucked and lurched up Heights Road, never quite finding that sweet spot between letting up the clutch and pushing down the gas. With each stall I would scream a string of obscenities at the Jeep. It was the car's fault, of course. The more I cursed, the harder Mom laughed. That just made me angrier, and more profane. It makes me feel a little better that years later, my sweet, beautiful, graceful sister Libby shouted even worse things at the Jeep when it was her turn to buck and lurch. Mom and I had gone through the same thing when she helped me with my eighth grade algebra homework. Textbooks flew across my bedroom.

Just as you had imagined when you bought it, the red Jeep was a cool, original car to drive that last year of high school. I was lucky to have it. I mean, what other car has a universal wave among its owners? Being a Jeep owner is like being in Skull and Bones—once you're tapped on the shoulder, you're in the club (except members of the Jeep Club are much less likely to become United States presidents or Supreme Court justices than the boys of Skull and Bones, and there's far less chanting and paddling).

The red Jeep took some punishment during that final year of high school. There was the time I slammed it into a Dumpster outside Benjamin Franklin Middle School when I rolled into the lot a little hot for a pickup basketball game. There were the many times during a thunderstorm when the process of putting the top on was just too daunting and I drove through the rain as puddles formed on the floor.

There was the time after our senior prom when a group of us drove up through the snow to Oswego, New York. Our prom was held in early March that year, with the idea being that keeping the big night out of the usual warm-weather month of June would prevent kids from getting drunk and driving to the Jersey Shore. So instead we drank and drove to upstate New York. When we arrived at the home in Oswego that some trusting soul had rented to a bunch of seventeen-year-olds, it was so snowy it was hard to make out the driveway. I drove the red Jeep right through the yard into a metal jungle gym set. I felt bad about that. As you might imagine, we lost our security deposit. It probably didn't help that we were also doing cannonballs into the hot tub in their carpeted living room. Seriously, though, who has a hot tub in the living room?

What with Dumpsters, jungle gyms, and topless rainstorms, the Jeep was ready for a rest by the time I went off to college. As I went south to Nashville, I left the red Jeep behind. We'd been inseparable. It was a little like saying goodbye to your high school girlfriend (mine came with me to college, so that was good). With its blazing red color and the good loud engine that revved while I forced it into gear, everyone always knew the Jeep and I were coming. We parted ways tearfully—or maybe the Jeep was just leaking coolant again.

When I returned the following summer, I put the red Jeep right back to work. As you know, Dad, I got a job as the delivery guy for a popular pizza joint in Ridgewood. In the interview they asked if I had a car. Technically I did. Luckily they didn't ask for specifics. A Jeep with no power steering, and shocks installed during Reagan's first term, is not the chariot you want for your home-delivered pizza. I bounced around Bergen County, New Jersey, with pizzas riding shotgun. By the time they reached their destinations, the hot cheese had adhered to the top of the box, leaving just tomato sauce on the crust itself. On more than a few occasions I quickly handed my customer a pizza and bolted back to the driveway before the product could be inspected. There was the occasional complaint, but far fewer than you'd expect for pizzas that were thrown around a bouncing army vehicle before they were delivered.

The Jeep and I really only saw each other during the summers for a while. Like a great thoroughbred put out to pasture, it appeared the CJ-7 was to live out the rest of its days comfortably, puttering around town, running errands, and remaining close to service stations at all times. But then one Christmas break, I decided I needed a car in Nashville. I certainly couldn't afford one, new or used, on the pizza tips, and you and Mom agreed the Jeep just wasn't up to the task of a fourteen-hour winter drive south. We looked very briefly into shipping it, but that would have cost thousands. I was out of options. So I walked to the garage in the backyard, threw up the door, and asked that old filly if she'd take one last ride with me. We were going to Music City, USA.

You and Mom rightly had grave concerns about the trip, but you knew I was going one way or another. Mom also knew this was not a one-man job, so she bravely volunteered to join me on this journey into the unknown. The nine-hundred-mile trek through six states would have been risky under the best conditions, but two days before we were to push off in the rusty Jeep with a vinyl roof, a big, nasty snowstorm rolled in. Meteorological records were broken, interstates were shut down, and states of emergency were declared. We drove right into the weather.

The Jeep crawled down I-81 carefully, flanked by snowdrifts and eighteen-wheelers flashing their hazard lights. Just as the sun went down on our first day, the headlights on the Jeep flickered and then went out completely. She had gone to sleep. We pulled off the highway somewhere in Pennsylvania and found a helpful mechanic who said he'd help us…when the part came in the next day. So Jody Geist and I spent the evening in a truck-stop diner sharing stories with our fellow road warriors. Even the big rig drivers thought we were nuts to be out there.

After a night in an off-brand motel, we woke up and found that, sure enough, the mechanic had found the part, God bless him. We were back in business…momentarily. Just as we started to hit a groove on Day Two of the Music City Odyssey, the accelerator went limp. You know, the thing that makes the car go. Not good. It would come back to life occasionally and we took one of those occasions to roll off the interstate to another service station. That's where we learned we were suffering from "gas line freeze." It was so bitterly cold outside (and inside our breezy Jeep) that the gas was freezing as it traveled to the engine. There was a solution that didn't require a part, but wasn't going to help us make good time. We had to stop every hour or so and let the red Jeep drink the sweet, sweet nectar of anti-freeze. So, like moonshiners, we loaded up the back of the Jeep with jugs of the stuff and pulled over to the narrow shoulder for a refill when it got thirsty.

Just as we'd perfected the routine, the Jeep made it clear one last time that it was not enjoying our voyage through the blizzard. Like Stephen King's Christine, the red Jeep began accelerating on its own. I had lost control. This could be the end. My poor mother had volunteered to crew the *Titanic*. The engine was revved all the way, all the time. I can't tell you now how we did it, but we managed to swing off the highway and glide into one more truck stop. Turns out the open throttle had frozen and stuck to another metal part in the engine. There was talk at that point of leaving the car right where it sat, forever. Maybe it was time to face reality and call Hertz. Perhaps we'd asked too much of the red Jeep this time. But how could we possibly leave it—a member of the family—behind, after all we'd been through in the dozen years since you laid down that seventy-seven hundred bucks and change?

I don't remember how we melted the ice on that throttle (a Bic lighter?), but we warmed up the Jeep enough to get her on the road again. When we finally sputtered into

Nashville, three days behind schedule, Mom and I kissed the ground like the Apollo 13 astronauts returning from the dark side of the moon. For the first time in its life, our red Jeep had a new home.

The Red Jeep's Last Stand

BILL

When the Jeep hobbled home from college a couple of years later, Libby got the keys. "Thanks a lot," she now says sarcastically. Well, we didn't want to spoil her with a car that was safe and operational.

Your mother had suffered enough, so I taught Libby to drive it; on a weekend, in a grade school parking lot, where children played. "You'd better clear out of here," I shouted to the Big Wheelers and hopscotch players. "We're gonna be doing some serious driving. No joke. You're not safe here. Or there, or even over there."

Libby punched the accelerator, the engine roared, the Jeep stayed put. She had it in neutral. The hard part of driving a stick shift, of course, is letting the clutch out gently while simultaneously and smoothly putting pressure on the accelerator.

This she did not do. Not the first, the second, or the tenth time, which resulted in the Jeep's buck-buck-bucking forward a few feet, then stopping. The kids loved the show, and no one was laughing harder than Libby. She has that great quality of finding almost everything, including humiliation, funny.

I told Libby I wanted her to learn to drive this hulking monster (Jeeps were bigger then) with the bad stick transmission and no power steering so that she'd be able to drive anything (including tanks and armored personnel carriers). She didn't buy it.

She finally mastered the vehicle, though, and drove it to school. It still *looked* cool, like brand-new stone-washed jeans with holes. I must admit the one big rusty hole beneath the driver's seat was somewhat unsettling. "And drafty," Libby added.

Now, when I say she drove it "to school" I really mean she drove it *toward* school. She'd routinely leave in the morning, then call ten minutes later to let Jody know where she'd broken down this time.

Fifteen years hence she tells me it was something of a "community car," meaning friends sometimes drove it during the school day. She'd go out to find the Jeep brimming with kids and who knows where they'd been or how many pedestrian casualties and fender benders they'd caused.

Only now does she also tell me that toward the end the red Jeep wouldn't go faster than forty miles per hour, which made midnight runs to McDonald's, requiring her to merge and drive on a road with cars traveling seventy miles per hour, hair-raising.

And, sadly, the days of taking the doors, roof, and windshield off were over. The hard top was rusted on, so snapping on the soft top and cruising around wasn't possible. The doors, too, were rusty and she couldn't pry them off. So the aging "red Jeep," nearing fifteen years old now, hard years, had slowed to half its speed, was not nearly the fun it used to be, and didn't react well in rain or cold. I can relate to that.

After all of this, she says now that the not-power steering made her a better, stronger basketball player, and also says, "I'll not go through life without a red Jeep of my own, I promise." It's the Geistian way.

P.S. I felt so badly about making her drive a broken-down hulk, crazy me goes out and buys her a fancy BMW! Two thousand bucks! "Save Big On Pre-pre-pre-Owned Cars and Trucks!"

Geist Date in History
September 12, 1987

Bill's collection of *New York Times* essays *City Slickers* is released. He holds a book party at the top of the Empire State Building at which twelve-year-old Willie meets Donald Trump. Like those who have had an audience with the Pope, Willie considers the audience with His Hugeness (pronounced "Uuuuugeness") the day that has informed every one thereafter.

Willie meets The Donald

Chapter 4

"Dad, this really sucks"

BILL

> *Give a boy a fish and he will wonder why. Teach a boy to fish and he will realize you don't know what you're talking about and will question everything you tell him forever. —Proverb*

I wanted to be a good father and teach you so many of the things my father never taught me: hunting, camping, fishing. But, like my father and his father before him, I had no clue how to do any of these things.

Bill shows off his (recently purchased?) fish

Willie learns from the Master

Willie proudly displays (someone else's?) fish

Yet I was determined to prune our family tree of ineptitude in outdoor activities. I'd grown up an observer, as had my father, a serious amateur photographer who taught the subject and who once owned a small country newspaper. An observer. But I wanted you, Willie, to know how to actually do things, well enough to enjoy them and to participate when and if you chose.

Camping wasn't going to work. In the army I slept out in the open on bare ground because it was such a pain in the ass to put up a tent. Hunting wasn't going to work either; I went once and rooted for the ducks.

It would have to be fishing, even though my only real experience had been at a water-filled hole created by construction of an interstate cloverleaf. An entrepreneur, probably trespassing on government lands, stocked the pond with perhaps the least desirable of all fish, the carp, and charged admission. My friends and I caught none but he gave us five on the way out and we hoisted them up triumphantly for a photograph.

I remember one morning at our Nantucket rental cottage when you were fifteen. I tiptoed into the dark bedroom where you were sleeping, naturally, at four thirty a.m., and stumbled over a flip-flop before reaching out to jostle your shoulder and whisper, "Son, it's time to go fishing."

"What?" you replied.

"Fishing, remember?"

"Dad," you said, half awake.

"Yes, Son?"

"Get out of my room."

I've never understood why fishing has to be at dawn.

Basketball, football, baseball—no other sports start at such a painful hour. It may be the fault of the fish. Perhaps genetic engineers will solve this problem in our, or your, lifetime. A large, colorful, easily mountable sport fish, stupid enough to go after fluorescent lures, skips breakfast and eats a big lunch.

We were to meet Phil, a genial, charming older man with lots of fishing equipment that he was willing to share, and at least a working knowledge of how to use it.

To avoid being rude to him, you got up.

We would be surf casting at a heavenly spot, Great Point, reachable by Jeep after we let some air out of the tires for the six-mile beach drive. In the dawn's early light, Phil gave us a brief casting demonstration and a couple of lures, then moved a safe distance away from us.

Problems arose. The two of us weren't casting far enough—like not far enough to hit the water. While reeling in I did hook a beer can just offshore and pretended I was doing my part to Save the Planet. On several occasions you and I entangled our lines and broke them. Our lines would pile up in a mess, like a bird's nest, on the reel.

But finally we did get into something of a rhythm, casting almost correctly, again and again. That was good. Except we weren't catching any fish. Others nearby brought in the occasional, notoriously inedible, bluefish. The preferred striped bass apparently weren't around, perhaps waiting for us to take our unappetizing, treble-hooked, psychedelic lures—how stupid do we think fish *are*?—and go home.

One of us, probably Phil, did catch a single blue. One fish for perhaps five hundred casts by the three of us. We took a picture.

There were further family fishing expeditions. We took a family vacation to Canada, where Uncle Bert had promised he would impart his extensive fishing knowledge to you and the rest of us. You, your mom, and I joined him in a small boat to go after muskie. Trophy fish. Bert wore an Orvis fishing vest, mark of a true pro, from which he removed a small box containing a silver lure that he said was a family heirloom. He tied it to the end of his line, reared back, and let fly. Out and out it sailed, a long, long, beautiful cast, unimpeded by the line, which had become detached from the free-flying heirloom. Gone.

One of us did hook a muskie and it was exciting until it had been reeled in to within two feet of the boat, whereupon Bert struck it hard with a paddle. He explained that muskies have sharp teeth and must be coldcocked so they won't bite. His wallop knocked the fish off the hook and it swam away. Your mother wound up making the only catch that day, an ugly suckerfish.

Unable to get a fish on the line, Uncle Bert spent the remainder of the voyage standing at the bow, smacking the water with the paddle in an attempt to KO the many fish swimming without fear close to the surface and close to the boat, in plain view, as if mocking us.

On later family outings, we've actually caught a few fish, but serious obstacles remain on our journey to become a true fishing family. For example, you, your sister, and I can't touch a flapping fish, let alone remove an ensconced hook from its mouth. That's up to your mother. My technique is to haul the fish aboard while it's still on the line, fling it into a cooler, close the top, and cut the line. If we have to touch one, we wear gardening gloves.

Somehow there does exist an unretouched photograph of you cleaning and filleting a fish after watching a rented video on how to do it. Perhaps, in this one area, I have achieved mild success in straining, if not breaking, the family's chain of ineptitude.

Back on that earlier outing with Phil in Nantucket, the three of us had been casting without so much as a nibble for over an hour. I could just barely make out your faint figure down the beach in the morning fog.

You called out, "Daaaad?"

"What is it, Son?"

"This reeeally sucks!"

"Yes it does, Son. Yes it does."

Willie and the Fishes

Yes, Dad, we've not-caught-fish in the cold waters of the Atlantic, the roaring rivers of Montana, the great lakes of Canada, and fishing holes across the American South. I've spent long days puking over the side of some of the Caribbean's finest fishing charters. Those outings sucked, every last one of them. So why did I enjoy them so much?

That foggy Nantucket morning may have been the first time I uttered the immortal phrase "Dad, this reeeally sucks!" during a father-son outing, but it certainly wasn't the last. "Dad, this reeeally sucks!" has since become short-hand for us. It's our way of stopping to identify a moment that we're enjoying hating together. Perverse as it may sound, we live for moments that suck—the ones where everything is terrible…and there's nowhere we'd rather be. It's a strange way of recognizing a father-son moment, I'll grant you that, but you may have noticed by now that we're a little strange.

"Dad, this reeeally sucks!" applies to a Sunday afternoon on the golf course after we've both sprayed our drives irre-trievably deep into the protected woodlands, or off the rear panel of a minivan passing on the road along the second fairway. Come to think of it, maybe it's not the activities that suck. Perhaps it's us.

"Dad, this reeeally sucks!" works nicely when whispered during a big, overwrought song-and-dance number at a Broadway show we've been roped into by Mom (who gets a lot more right than wrong on the theater-roping, by the way).

Same goes for a modern art installation in SoHo where a guy has painted one black stripe on a giant white canvas and wants us all to bow to the genius of his minimalist sim-plicity. In that case we might just give each other a brief, nonverbal look and nod of agreement that the afternoon has taken a turn down Reeeally Sucks Lane, so as not to offend those who are "appreciating" the work.

There is the occasional, more emphatic variation on the classic. Let's say we've just spent a half hour during a fam-ily car trip at a down-market local roadside attraction—generally the only kind where we stop. That might earn a gleeful "Dear *Lord*, this sucks! I mean, wow! Man alive!" I'm looking at you, "Geographic Center of the United States" in Lebanon, Kansas: You're such a terrible "attraction" that we just love you.

So when I shouted those four words—"Dad, this reeeally sucks!"—to you in the predawn surf, with the lovely gentleman Phil Bash out of earshot, it was an honest observation, yes, but it also was the beginning of a lifelong connection between two guys who were starting to see the world in the same funny way. The worse the better, we always seem to think. It's the Tao of Geist.

I veered off into the sentimental for a moment there. My apologies. It won't happen again. So, yeah, we suck at fishing. That's not to say we *never* catch fish. There were plenty of times after that first morning that we went out and caught loads of bluefish off a boat staffed by people who knew what they were doing. Those big hauls just encouraged us, though. Fishing is like golf that way—you have one good day and you're convinced you could be great at it. So you go out and buy the gear, tie the knots, study the tides, pack the cooler, and learn the lingo to create the illusion of competence. To trick yourself into thinking that a beige vest with pockets full of sharp equipment makes you...a Fisherman.

Bill Fisher Tackle is a great little shop in Nantucket where each summer we'd buy anew all those trappings, starting with that season's Bill Fisher T-shirt. With a color that changed every year and a simple logo on the front pocket, the Bill Fisher T-shirt signaled, we thought, that we meant business. That we were part of the fishing community. That we knew all the spots. That we'd be back soon, ladies, with a trunk full of blues, so just have the grill runnin'. Turns out it signaled that we were seasonal tourists with twenty dollars to waste on a T-shirt, but I'll be damned if I didn't parade around that island in my T-shirt as if I were Poseidon, God of the Sea. "Let's mount up, Dad. I hear the blues are runnin' out at the Barrels," I'd say with unwarranted confidence. I had the T-shirt on.

There's a variation of "the Barrels" in just about every town on earth with a river, a creek, a lake, a pond, a bay, or an ocean. It always feels good to say something like "Stripers are hittin' hard through Plum Gut." Whether the information is accurate is hardly the point. You're in the game. You're throwing the lingo around. You're having long conversations about worms. That's why you fish, man. The fish themselves? They have those at Whole Foods.

Our first real fishing vessel is a story in itself. As we started spending more and more time on Shelter Island, New York, Dad bought a green 1973 Lyman inboard. A really great boat in its day. The last year Lymans rolled off the production line was '73, so ours was considered "a classic." As anyone with a "classic" automobile can attest, *classic* is often a euphemism for "worthless, beat-up piece of shit." Age does not always carry with it classic-ness. Now, "piece of shit" is a little strong for the boat we had, but it certainly performed like a relic of the Nixon years.

If you wanted to turn the boat, for example, you had to go ahead and budget a solid minute or so. Pull that wheel left, have a sandwich, throw down a beer, catch up with friends and relatives in the bow area, and by then the ol' Lyman was ready to make that wide bend to the port side.

To dock the boat was to reenact the final dramatic moments of the RMS *Titanic.* With my dad at the wheel and me up front, I'd turn and yell back, "Iceberg straight ahead!" As women and children scrambled to the rescue boats and the orchestra played on deck to maintain calm, Dad and I would bring the RMS *Lyman* home and tie her up, generally with healthy chunks removed from her bow. Nothing that couldn't be repaired with some duct tape and a black Sharpie.

We hung in with the old girl for years until one fateful, smoke-filled evening during an otherwise delightful booze cruise with guests. As we leaned back with the summer wind in our hair, carving up the tame waves of the Long Island Sound, drinks in hand, life in front of us, smoke began to billow from the console that sat in the middle of the boat and housed the inboard motor. We powered down as the passengers began to look politely for the nearest personal flotation device. We flipped open the top of the console and the smoke poured out. It appeared she was about to blow. To make matters worse, the engine cover was lined with some variety of seventies-era fire retardant that surely had been banned for decades and actually aided in the billowing. Automatic fire extinguishers went off. There are conflicting accounts of that evening, but I maintain my sister, Libby, abandoned ship, like Kate Winslet into the North Atlantic. A total disaster, and sadly the end of the green Lyman. Again, the boat "reeeally sucked," and we liked it that way. I'm starting to think that there may be something wrong with us.

It was on a better day aboard the Lyman that my dad first uttered the phrase, "Follow the birds, Will! Follow the birds!" A perfect example of lingo we'd heard some-where, and that made some sense logically, I guess (the birds know where the fish are, right?), but probably meant nothing. That line never fails to make me laugh. "Follow the birds!" It's especially funny when there isn't a bird in the sky. Instead of finding where the fish are ourselves, we prefer driving around in a smoky boat belting fishing cli-chés across the open water. "Follow the birds!"

My one signature fishing move—one that actually does work, believe it or not—was developed and perfected on a fishing trip with friends in Plaquemines Parish, Louisi-ana, last year, during the bachelor party of my good friend Parker. He decided against the clichéd "hookers and black-jack" bachelor affair in Vegas, and instead led us deep into southern Louisiana in search of redfish. About as far down as you can go, actually, to desolate areas almost completely wiped out by Hurricane Katrina and dotted with only the odd trailer or hulking oil refinery.

We stayed in bunk beds in an old fishing lodge in Buras, where a sweet old lady made us dinner each night. When we asked about the best local bars to hit for a night of bachelors' debauchery, we were told, and I quote, "Don't you boys go to these bars. You go in there, you might not come out." Vegas has its inherent dangers, but you gen-erally aren't murdered in the bars there because you're a fancy boy from the city. So we fished. We ate, we drank, we played poker...and we fished.

After a slow start on Saturday morning, I caught fire.

Every time I threw the line out, it came back with a good-size keeper. Finally my friend Pearson turned and asked me for my secret. As if I have a secret. I made one up quickly. I leaned in close as though I were the keeper of ancient fishing wisdom, and told him about the Shrimp Cocktail Method. Instead of just slapping a scrap of shrimp on the lure, I artfully arranged two full shrimp on the hook and lured them in.

While my fellow fishermen were slapping the shrimp on their hooks haphazardly and expecting the redfish to bite, I was *presenting* the shrimp to the fish as if it were an appetizer at Le Bernardin. One shrimp is fine, I guess, but why not offer a two-piece draped handsomely over the hook? If you can find a seaweed garnish, great. If you want to bring along a lemon wedge, that's your business. Is it gonna cost you a little more? Sure. It's the price we pay out on the water.

Sure enough, with just a little presentation, Pearson started crushing reds himself. From that moment Pearson, and dare I say the fishing community at large, stopped laughing at the rod-and-reel skills of Willie Geist. He had given them the Shrimp Cocktail Method.

Dad, I'm almost glad you weren't there that day to see me reeling in all those big, beautiful fish. I broke our tacit father-son agreement by actually *catching* fish. It won't happen again.

Geist Date in History

July 15, 1982

In town for a reunion, the Geist and Lewis (Jody's side) families stay at a Holiday Inn convenient to the Indianapolis home of patriarch, and member of the Hockey Hall of Fame, Herbie Lewis.

One morning Bill walks into the hotel restaurant and spots Aunt Sharon having breakfast. The restaurant is decorated in old-fashioned farm style, wholesome and homey. There are pictures of antique tractors on the walls and maybe a scythe or two. The curtains are blue-and-white-checked, matching the waitresses' outfits.

Jody, Grandpa George, uncles Mike, Herb, and Bert, Bill, Willie, and Aunt Sharon at family favorite Steak 'n Shake

Sharon goes through the breakfast buffet line, where a fairly prominent NO SHARING sign is posted. Bill joins her and the waitress comes right over asking "Coffee?" She is a pleasant-looking woman of about sixty-five years—looks like Mrs. Orville Redenbacher. She asks if Bill plans to enjoy the breakfast buffet, but he declines: "Just coffee's fine, ma'am."

During the course of conversation with Sharon, Bill reaches over and takes a slice of bacon from her plate. Two minutes later he takes a second.

The pleasant, grandmotherly waitress has seen enough of the flagrant buffet sharing. She walks over, leans down, her mouth to Bill's ear, and says softly:

"I seen what you's a-doin', you little shit-ass."

Her words become part of the Geist lexicon forevermore.

Chapter 5

A Sledgehammer Christmas

BILL

O ne memorable Christmas, about one hundred presents had been opened during the rowdy celebration, a good fifteen or so by you alone, Willie. Three remained: locked—nay, sealed, entombed—in the trunk of my company car, a gray-blue Buick Skylark parked in our driveway.

A few days earlier, another vehicle had bumped into the back of the Skylark. Nothing serious, but on this Christmas day the trunk wouldn't open. Uncle Mike, Uncle

Willie's first Christmas

Herb, and I went outside on a manly mission to rescue the gifts.

We fiddled with the trunk key for a while, pushing it in slowly, quickly, forcefully, every which way. No go. We tried sitting on the trunk and bouncing up and down. Nothing.

More extreme measures would be required. Mike began phase two of the operation by tapping the trunk lock with a hammer, gently at first and finally with nail-pounding force. To no avail.

Cursing ensued on Jesus's birthday.

Then the situation began to turn ugly. We weren't thinking clearly, our senses altered by too many trips to the punch bowl (the family eggnog recipe: one part bourbon, one part rum, one part grocery store eggnog, topped with a festive dash of nutmeg and more rum). The nog was complemented with tidbits of an edible fungus Willie's uncle Herb had presumably happened upon during a stroll through a forest. He's always had a way with, uh, "natural supplements."

When Herb came out of the house brandishing a very large screwdriver, I said, calmly, "It's a little late for that."

While he'd been in the basement looking for tools, I'd gone to the garage, where I found a sledgehammer, which I used to deliver several blows to the target area. This while the fire crackled, Bing Crosby sang, and children laughed inside, oblivious to the demolition taking place in the driveway.

When even *the sledgehammer* proved insufficient, I fetched the heavy steel wedge that I always used in conjunction with the sledgehammer to split logs. I delivered several blows in and around the formidable lock mechanism, as did each of the uncles. Nothing. Unfortunately, by this point there was a good deal of collateral damage to the vehicle.

Using a crowbar, we pried open one side of the trunk, but that wasn't sufficient, so we yanked it up a few inches more. Now we could glimpse the gifts, but they were on the opposite side of the trunk, so we pried that open too. We removed the unharmed gifts and triumphantly took them inside, leaving behind a wreck of a car that, from the rear, looked less like a Buick than a butterfly.

"Great Christmas," Uncle Herb said, upon leaving the celebration. "I never dreamed you'd let us take a sledgehammer to your car!"

~

Company cars were serviced at a small garage in the city. I'd stopped in before Christmas to tell them the trunk wouldn't open. They said it was no big deal, gave me an estimate of ninety-five dollars, and said they'd fix it right after the holiday.

So the day after Christmas I drove to work in New York in my winged vehicle, all the way drawing looks of "What is that?" and "What could have possibly caused something like that?" I parked it at the garage, placed the nincty-five-dollar estimate on the dashboard, and walked away. The garage and my employer haggled for many weeks over the cost of this rear-end collision, everyone happy that nobody had been hurt.

No one seems to remember what those three gifts were,

but their rescue lives on in family lore. I'm sorry you had to witness that, Willie.

Willie Postscript

No apology necessary. I remember thinking it was cool that our gray family car, with its trunk butterflied up on both sides, looked like the silver DeLorean from *Back to the Future*. I guess I didn't realize how the Skylark got that way. Or that it belonged to the *New York Times*.

Geist Date in History

December 25, 1994

On Christmas morning, a life-size fiberglass cow appears in the front yard of the Geist home, wrapped in a bow. It's a surprise gift from Jody to Bill, since he's admired it in an L.A. antique shop for years. But the next morning the cow is gone. Stolen. On Christmas! After receiving notification of an expensive missing plastic cow, the police in Ridgewood, New Jersey, chuckle...and then begin their forensic investigation. The cow is returned by neighborhood pranksters the next day in true suburban fashion—with a bottle of Chardonnay and an apology. Nearly two decades later, the cow is down a tail and an ear, but still lives in Bill and Jody's yard, baffling all who see her. Fortunately, no attempts have been made to steal the Elvis bust on a pedestal in the dining room.

Bill's plastic cow unfazed by
Willie's naked son, George

Chapter 6

Yuletide at Grandpa George's Zoo

BILL

S ince you were only two and a half at the time, I thought you might like to hear further details about one of your first Christmas eve celebrations at Grandpa George's

Young Willie off to
fight another blaze

Willie and sister Libby
defy orders to smile for
a Christmas card shot

Willie surrounded by his trucks,
Christmas 1977

house—if only so you can pass along the rich family lore to future generations. Also it might help in psychotherapy.

You know what they say: People make a party. And your mother's Lewis side of the family has an all-star lineup of revelers: the untamed rapscallion and unlicensed pharmacist Uncle Herb (Jody's brother); the agent provocateur Uncle Mike (Jody's brother); the riotous, eccentric Aunt Lindy (Jody's sister); and the unprofessional comedian Uncle Bert (Lindy's husband).

George's second wife, Jeanne, was our hostess that night, with her three vampy daughters, one of whom had brought along her better half, an alleged drug dealer. Plus random invitees including fellow commuter train riders and a uniformed conductor.

A festive holiday punch heightened the merriment. Atop the portable dishwasher sat a large punch bowl full of what may have started out as wassail, though I doubt it, but turned into something akin to liquid napalm as each new arrival added a flammable intoxicant to the concoction.

The ambiance? Avant-garde decor fit for a surrealist's ball: Live birds fluttered about the house; "show" chickens crapped here and there; a couple of dogs roamed in search of hors d'oeuvres, and a handful of hermit crabs were sprinkled through the shag carpeting.

To appreciate all this, you really had to know George, but I suspect no one ever fully did.

He grew up athletic, handsome, and funny. Beginning in a boyhood that would last a lifetime he held a keen interest in animals, both domestic and exotic, and there were always some of each free-range in his home. He had forty fish tanks in the basement, with varieties Chicago's Shedd Aquarium envied. He spent countless hours after work with his sleeves rolled up, hands and arms in the tanks, feeding the fish frozen brine shrimp, which was kept in the freezer, and somehow always seemed to mingle with the ice cream. And every day he came up the steps mourning another loss.

He was the first person I ever heard of who'd rescued a greyhound from a racetrack, something he'd begun doing in the 1950s. The family dog, when I met George, was the general idea of an English sheepdog named Trouble. Animal Control had become so tired of chasing him that it finally gave up and granted Trouble amnesty.

Uncle Mike and Aunt Lindy swear their father once had a bear staked out in the backyard. Uncle Herb remembers it in the basement, along with a young alligator. And there were the pair of monkeys, whom Jody's mother, Edi, ordered him to take to a zoo. He did, but during the trip the monkeys escaped and passersby got quite a show as George chased them down.

His Christmas eve parties involved no caroling (howling, yes) or cookie decorating. I'd come from a low-key (i.e., normal) family where we might go over to Aunt Hazel's house for tea, gingerbread, and carols 'round the piano. Or perhaps spend Christmas eve in front of our tree, exchanging modest gifts with Aunt E.G. and her three girls.

At the Lewis annual Glorification of the Newborn King Blowout, Herb kept the Christmas music—e.g., "Santa's Got A Brand New Bag" by James Brown—at full volume, though the din of shouting and laughter overrode even that. Any attempt to put you, a toddler, to bed was shouted down with accusations that we were "overprotective."

Of course, no one else in the room had kids, which at times did have its advantages. As the first grandchild, you received thirteen toy fire trucks of all sizes and sirens. Others of us weren't so lucky. One year George gave everyone "pony" après-ski boots with long white hair. Another Christmas he gave all the men red polka-dot polyester shirts that proved such a hit, he gave them the next year. Yet another year I had put ice skates on my Christmas list and when I opened his gift, there they were! I was astonished he had finally given me a real gift. Upon further review, I found that the skates were used, which would have been fine had they not been two and a half sizes too small.

Once George outdid himself, giving Uncle Herb a "new" car! He'd won the vehicle in a poker game. George was practiced at poker, having honed his skills in decades of serious games on the commuter train and all-night games above the local police station, with the chief at the table. I went with Mike and George to pick up the new car, which was a mammoth (now extinct), light-beige, fifteen-year-old station wagon. George started her up, which was encouraging. He operated the wipers, lights, and other accessories before hitting the automatic tailgate window opener. The window began lowering but suddenly developed an ominous grinding sound before exploding into a million pieces. Mike and I doubled over with laughter. George was not happy with us. Mike and Herb did use the car, but the fumes were overpowering, almost as if the exhaust pipe were hooked into the air-conditioning system.

That's just one of the extraordinary tales in the "George vs. the Machine" series. There's the pre-owned Cadillac convertible story, in which George took a client to dinner: When he dropped the client off at home, the passenger door would not open, and George had to pull him out through the window. Yes, George had clients, and lots of them. He was a highly successful commodities trader.

And there was the silver Chevy convertible, which was packed like a can of sardines with the family of six, its top down, from Chicago to Boynton Beach, Florida. It was August. George made stops at brackish ponds along the way to wade in and net a rare fish or perhaps catch a live three-legged snapping turtle, which he would put in the backseat with the kids.

But I digress. Back to the Christmas eve party, where someone was, ill-advisedly, taking photos. When the three temptress stepdaughters, by now three sheets to the wind, posed, unfortunately one had her bared left breast staring directly at the lens.

Uncle Herb was cleaning up, stoking the fireplace with

gift box after gift box and tons of wrapping paper, to the point that the flames set fire to the mantel (damned near to the reputed drug dealer, who was napping with his head on the hearth).

When the blaze was 75 percent contained, Herb said he was going out to "buy eggnog" accompanied by one of the stepsisters. There must have been quite a tussle at the dairy case because both returned disheveled. Your mom tried to put you to bed in the least cacophonous bedroom, where she found on the pillow not sugarplums to dance in your sweet little head but a show chicken nesting.

Grandpa George would later retire to Florida and surround himself with talking parrots and plants, much of the flora growing to fifty times the size they would have back in Chicago. His house became almost completely concealed and rumors spread that his triple-canopy yard was inhabited by a tribe of previously un-contacted natives.

He returned north only twice, both times to see you play football and basketball, Willie. Then he went back home to Florida and disappeared into his own personal jungle paradise.

Geist Date in History
October 31, 1980

In the year of the release of *The Empire Strikes Back*, Willie proudly steps out for Halloween in a full kick-ass Chewbacca costume. The cheap, easy way would have been to pay ten bucks at Kmart for a plastic getup with a flimsy, inauthentic mask. The Jody Geist way is to labor over the sewing machine for days, piecing together yards of fabric and real Wookiee fur to make the perfect homemade Chewbacca costume. Not super-breathable, but that's hardly the point. Willie dominates Halloween because Jody Geist is the best.

Willie in Jody's homemade Chewbacca costume

Chapter 7

Baseball, Fathers, Sons... and All That

WILLIE

The public line on why we moved from Chicago to New Jersey when I was five years old, Dad, has always been

Willie in the Yankees farm system

Willie and family after another win for the Ridgewood Maroons

The mean-mugging football phenom

that you were lured East by a job offer from the *New York Times*. Now that the statute of limitations is up, the truth can be told: You just didn't want to raise me as a Cubs fan. You always said it constituted child abuse under the laws of the state of Illinois and it wouldn't happen on your watch. Some thirty-five years later, history smiles on that decision.

It's not just that you got us out of the baseball ghetto, it's that you took us to the fanciest neighborhood in the game. At the time we moved to the New York area, the Yankees were coming off a pair of World Series titles in 1977 and '78. Of course, they went dark for a decade or so there in the eighties and early nineties, but we were rewarded for our patience in the era of Saint Jeter. Meanwhile, the Cubs continue to batter the hearts of children across the greater Chicagoland area and mock the very concept of faith. The Cubbies last won the World Series a month before Bill Taft knocked off William Jennings Bryan in the 1908 presidential race.

Having escaped the death grip of the Chicago Cubs, I became a Yankee fan. A big one. When we went on summer vacations, I wrote postcards to my favorite player, Dave Winfield. I'd sit down and send Big Dave a message from Cape Cod, letting him know about my escapades at the beach and my triumphs on the mini golf course. Winfield likely had been wondering where I was. I'm not sure, Dad, if you ever mailed any of those postcards, but I did once get in the mail a signed photograph of #31. That confirmed for me that Winnie (or the member of the Yankees organization who had stamped his autograph) was out there hearing my cheers.

In backyard games with you, I imitated every nuance of Winfield's batting stance, committed to memory from hours of Yankee games watched on New York's WPIX, channel 11. The long dig in the batter's box dirt with the back foot while asking the umpire for a time-out. The steadying of the loose-fitting helmet with a hand on top of the head. And, of course, the aggressive adjustment of the cup. I wasn't wearing a cup in the backyard, of course, so I'm sure my own adjustment struck the neighbors—and perhaps you, Dad—as a little odd.

Some of my favorite early baseball memories are of sitting in the living room with you, watching those Yankee games and studying the announcers almost as much as we studied the players on the field. Our favorite always and forever was the great Phil Rizzuto, known as "Scooter." A Yankee great as a player, Scooter became a folk hero in the broadcast booth. He was best known for his excited "Holy cow!" call, but it was his nightly endearing gaffe or long, tangential tale that you and I looked forward to most.

One night, as WPIX came back from a commercial break showing an overhead shot of traffic on the George Washington Bridge, Scooter informed his longtime partner in the booth Bill White that he was going to have to leave early to beat the traffic out of the ballpark. And he did. Another night, as the rain began to fall in the middle of the game, Scooter told White he had to run downstairs to roll up the windows on the car. Again, it wasn't shtick. He left the broadcast booth to roll up the windows on his car. We miss Scooter.

Meanwhile I used the Channel 11 graphics package as

a stall tactic for bedtime. You'll recall that as Mom tried like hell to get me to go to bed in the middle of a Yankee game, I would tell her I just had to see the Yankees hit one more time. Then, of course, I had to see if pitcher John "the Count" Montefusco got out of the top of the next inning. When he did and you reached to turn off the TV to support Mom, I'd shout every time without fail, "I wanna see the due-ups!" The "due-ups" being the list of the next three hitters coming to bat as the broadcast goes to commercial break. It's a visual and verbal tease: "Due up for the Yankees...Don Mattingly, Dave Winfield, and Mike Pagliarulo!" It was a vicious cycle. If I saw the "due-ups," I had a name that meant I needed to watch the next inning—"Dad! Mattingly is up next inning!" You left the TV on. The cycle repeated itself. I got a lot of extra baseball out of those due-ups.

The theme music for the Yankee broadcasts on WPIX became my personal anthem. When Mom forced me to take piano lessons in the third grade—I suspect she was beginning to worry about my singular fascination with sports and their announcers—I agreed to see the teacher on one condition: The first song I learned would be the WPIX Yankee song. The teacher said she didn't know that one. She was dead to me right then and there, but I humored Mom. I held up a crappy little Fisher-Price tape recorder to the TV set during the next night's game to record the song. I played it for the piano teacher at my next lesson and instructed her to teach me. She wanted Beethoven and I wanted Scooter. My piano career ended shortly thereafter.

When you live in New York, you're supposed to pick

either the Yankees or the Mets. One or the other. Mets fans tend to hate the Yankees, but Yankee fans are not as intense about their feelings in the other direction. There's a bit of a paternalistic element to it—"Come on, who hates the Mets? They're adorable." I never hated the Mets. In fact, I loved many of their players. As a Little League first baseman, I had Keith Hernandez as my idol. Remember, Dad, how I copied all his crafty little tricks? Like straddling first base to hold a runner on and sneaking up right on top of a hitter when he squared to bunt?

Although Yankees fans, we followed that incredible 1986 Mets season closely. When they made it to the World Series, we had to go. Plus, they were playing the Red Sox. It was important that the Sox not win and bring even an ounce of joy to the great Commonwealth of Massachusetts. I'll never forget being in the kitchen of the house we had just moved into that October of '86, hitting redial on the phone to try to get through to some hotline for tickets. (Remember when we did stuff like hitting redial on hotlines to get tickets to things?) At some point, somehow, we got through and got two seats to Game One. You and I drove our red Jeep to Flushing, Queens, parked her out on a desolate backstreet in a maze of auto repair and tire shops behind the old Shea Stadium. It was New York in the 1980s, so we just locked it up and assumed it would be gone when we returned. Well worth it to see this game.

After the infamous Bill Buckner Game Six, we went on a mission to get into Game Seven. I can't remember which kidney you sold for tickets, Dad, but it was a fair swap, and you're still struggling along with us today. The Mets won, and the Jeep went un-stolen. It was a time of change in New York.

I loved the experience of being at a ball game with all those people from every corner of New York and New Jersey. I remember as a kid going to the men's room with you in places like Shea or grungy old Yankee Stadium, or downright dangerous Giants Stadium, standing in line under a cloud of cigarette smoke as towering men with deep voices shouted obscenities at each other. The floor was wet with beer, water, and piss. Guys got into fights. Over what? I wondered. These were men. Real men. Someday I'll be a man, I thought. Those bathrooms had an air of danger that I loved and aspired to. Nowadays you get a Swedish massage and read the Style section of the *Times* on an iPad embedded in the wall while you stand at the urinal. I miss those smoky, shitty old stadiums.

Madison Square Garden was another one of those joints. You and I rooted for the Knicks, and worshiped Bernard King. He was a quick-release scoring machine. Just as I did with Winfield in baseball, I mimicked Bernard's every move in our backyard and on the playground. Remember when you and Mom met him once at Wyckoff Lighting in Jersey? Guy enjoys a nice fixture, just like the rest of us. To you and me, Dad, Bernard King will always be "Buh-nard Keeng." If Scooter was our favorite baseball announcer, the MSG Network's Butch Beard was our basketball guy. The great Marv Albert deserves all the praise he gets as the long-time Knicks play-by-play man (*"Ree-JECTED by Ewing!!!"*), but we always had a soft spot for Butch. His Kentucky accent ever present, Beard pronounced Bernard King "Buh-nard

Keeng." He also talked about strong players having "strenth" (no *g*) and successful ones being "suh-sess-ful." Putting it all together, you might hear our man Butch Beard say after a powerful drive to the basket, "Buh-nard Keeng has the strenth to be suhsessful."

One of the great days of our Geist sporting lives was the June afternoon when NBA commissioner David Stern announced on national television that the Knicks would receive the first pick in the 1985 NBA Draft. That meant we were getting the most fearsome college basketball player to come along in a generation: the great Patrick Ewing. We watched at Uncle Herb and Aunt Sharon's house in Connecticut while visiting their newborn son Herbie. We jumped and screamed at the news. Patrick was born unto us. It was like being present at the manger, although Ewing delivered considerably fewer championships than Jesus (aka Jordan).

As for college sports, I was born with Illini blood. Born, raised, and educated as you were in Champaign, Illinois, I'm pretty sure you didn't leave the city limits until you were twenty-three, Dad...after your *fifth* year of college. You met Mom at the University of Illinois. Grandma Marge, your wonderful mother and one of my best buddies through childhood, lived in Champaign until she died. U of I was our school. The Fighting Illini were our team. The walls of my bedroom in Ridgewood, New Jersey—not a hotbed of Big Ten activity—were covered with orange-and-blue Illinois wallpaper bearing the team's mascot, Chief Illiniwek. That's commitment.

I spent weeks of my summers back in Champaign with

Grandma Marge, attending Lou Henson's basketball camp at the U of I. Henson was the head basketball coach at Illinois, known for winning, but also for his folksiness and comb-over hairstyle known as "the Lou do." Lou would make token appearances at the summer camp's dining hall, chatting up "youngsters" with banter like, "Hello. Looks like you fellas have got some dessert." You can see why he was a master recruiter.

I was a nonresidential camper, staying at Grandma Marge's place. She made me grilled cheese every day and stocked the refrigerator with Popsicles. We ate dinner and played cards at night. It was heaven in central Illinois. Every morning I'd slip on my Lou Henson Basketball Camp T-shirt and Grandma Marge would drive me in her Buick to the Bromley Hall dorm on campus. This was twenty-five years ago, so the fact that she ripped cigarettes the whole way with the windows rolled up didn't even faze me.

The only other sports team that followed me from your home state of Illinois, Dad, was the Chicago Bears. And that was attributable less to their dominance during the 1980s and more to the sublime "Super Bowl Shuffle" video they made during their 1985 championship season. If you haven't seen "The Super Bowl Shuffle," performed by the Chicago Bears Shufflin' Crew, please take a brief moment now to review it online and then come right back.

The Bears brazenly recorded that song and accompanying video three months *before* they won the Super Bowl. It became such a phenomenon that it wound up on the

Billboard Hot 100 list and hilariously was nominated for
a Grammy in the category of Best Rhythm and Blues Performance by a Duo or Group (the rapping Bears football
team lost to Prince). "The Super Bowl Shuffle" was the
headlining gift of my Christmas 1985. Aunt Lindy and
Uncle Bert bought me a copy. I watched it until every
mumbled Richard Dent lyric and terrible Gary Fen-
cik dance move were burned into my ten-year-old
consciousness. It was my pre-Internet, pre-YouTube intro-
duction to the wonders of ironically great pop culture
moments.

I remained a Bears fan, and have committed to mem-
ory all the lyrics of their 1985 hit video, in which Willie
"I'm as Smooth as a Chocolate Swirl" Gault, "L.A. Mike"
Richardson, and "Mama's Boy" Otis Wilson mesmerized
with their cool. Backup quarterback Steve Fuller horrified
with his offbeat dancing and big, toothy grin. And
William "The Refrigerator" Perry was brought in to shut
the whole thing down, rapping in the song's final verse:
You're lookin' at the Fridge, I'm the rookie/I may be large, but
I'm no dumb cookie.

There are lines from "The Super Bowl Shuffle" that are
to this day shorthand for Dad and me. Richard Dent's "We
love to play for the world's best fans/You betta start makin'
ya Super Bowl plans" can be used to indicate preparation
for any event or holiday. As in: "Dad, Christmas is in two
weeks...*you betta start makin' ya Super Bowl plans.*"

Before you dismiss my many hours spent with "The
Super Bowl Shuffle" VHS tape as the depressing sign of a
wasted childhood, I would point you to a moment on live

national television when my total-immersion "Super Bowl Shuffle" training paid off. A few years ago, the writer Jeff Pearlman was a guest on *Morning Joe*. He was there to talk about his new Walter Payton book, *Sweetness*. Near the end of the interview, "The Super Bowl Shuffle" came up, and so too did the moment for which I'd been waiting a lifetime. An impromptu sing-along broke out and I busted out a verse I'd been holding in my back pocket for a quarter of a century. For a brief moment there on morning television, my life made sense, all thanks to the Grammy-nominated Chicago Bears Shufflin' Crew.

Little League and Beyond

My own athletic career is a matter of public record. In 1992, Bill Geist wrote a book called *Little League Confidential*, a memoir about coaching me and my sister, Libby, through suburban youth baseball and softball. Dad, you changed the names of our friends and neighbors, but we still got dirty looks in the aisles of the Grand Union grocery store for years after. Thanks for that. The book became a huge best seller and remains, for many people, the bible of over-zealous parenting, whether in sports, ballet, or the math bowl. With apologies to the apostles, it's much funnier than the Bible.

You mined for material during your years as skipper of any number of teams named for Ridgewood, New Jersey, retailers. My very first baseball team was River City Graphics. I was in second grade. All the imaginary games I'd played in the backyard with you, and the real ones I'd watched grown men play on television, came to life. I wasn't pretending anymore to be Dave Winfield in the batter's box or Rickey Henderson on the base paths. I was hitting live pitching and running the bases with real people trying to get me out. There were unnecessary slides into every base, and diving catches on routine plays—grass and dirt stains all over my green shirt and gray baseball pants. There were stirrup socks, colorful wristbands, and batting gloves sticky from the tape on the bats. There was infield chatter and gratuitous spitting. There were gum and sunflower seeds. There was mud knocked out of cleats with the end of a twenty-eight-inch aluminum bat. There were looks down the third base line to a coach signaling God knows what to a second grader. There were high fives after a home run and kicked dirt after a strikeout. There was winning and losing. There was ice cream after the game. It was thrilling. I counted the days between games—one during the week, one on Saturday.

I can still see the cursive writing on our green hats that first season: "River City Graphics." Do you remember that, Dad? The other teams settled for standard, league-issue block lettering because they, of course, were not sponsored by one of the area's leading graphic design firms. Beyond the inherent local prestige, the benefits of playing for, say, Sealfons department store, where the ladies of Ridgewood, New Jersey, shopped for sweater sets and undergarments, were less obvious. It's one thing to play for a pizza joint, but the kids who played for John J. Feeney and Sons Funeral Home (always black uniforms, naturally) didn't bother to inquire about freebies.

Over the course of my Little League career I played for Tarvin Realtors (where my mom later became a star agent), Ridgewood Hardware, and Renato's Pizza. Fortunately, I never had to suit up for the Ridgewood Corset Shop.

That Renato's Pizza squad was one of the greatest ever to grace a Little League field, if you don't mind my saying. The real secret to our success was our coach, Jim Hansen. Dr. James Hansen, I should say—as in the world-renowned climatologist who pioneered the concept of global warming. By day he testified before Congress about climate change. By night he taught us how to turn double plays. Amazing guy. How many NASA climatologists do you think have batting cages in the backyards of their homes? Dr. Hansen did. I wish I'd had the presence of mind back then to pick his brain about the future of the planet, but we mostly talked about increasing my bat speed through the hitting zone.

Dad, you were a good coach. You were not, to my knowledge, an astrophysicist, or really a nuts-and-bolts baseball technician, as a Little League coach. In fact, most of the lessons I took away from you about the game had to do with running a draft. In *Little League Confidential,* you laid out some important rules every coach should practice in the draft room. One of your first priorities, you said, is to draft a kid with a "hot mom." Even if it's a long season on the diamond—and it's likely to be if the only "talent" you're looking for is in the players' mothers—at least you have that mom sitting up the first base line in her folding beach chair to keep morale up. Your second rule was to draft a kid with a swimming pool for the postseason party. Funny, you never heard coaching wisdom like that from Vince Lombardi or John Wooden. You were an innovator.

You coached some of my basketball teams too. You spotted my talent—and my height—early on. Remember this family gem? On December 1, 1984, after my first organized basketball game, you rushed to your job in the *New York Times* newsroom. Instead of writing the story you were supposed to file for the paper, you wrote the following:

GEIST PACES NETS TO WIN IN HOOP OPENER

Ridgewood, NJ, Dec. 1—Willie Geist poured in 16 points today to lead the Ridgewood Nets to a 24–13 scrubbing of Ridgewood Auto Wash.

In this first game of the Biddy Basketball season, the Nets led the defensive battle 10–7 at halftime, but opened it up in the third quarter to polish off the Auto Wash five.

Fans and officials were stunned to learn that this was the first cage tilt ever for Geist, a lanky 4'11½" pivot man, who took to the hardwood like a starving beaver and hit the first six points for the Nets.

He electrified the standing-room-only crowd (regrettably there was just one bench and a couple of folding chairs for fans) with his prowess in every phase of the game. He controlled the tip on several jump balls, swept the boards clean and continually tickled the twines with his patented five-foot bank shots.

He netted seven deuces and two charity tosses. Hammered in bloody nose alley, Geist stepped to the stripe and calmly hit nothing but net, swishing his only two free throw attempts.

Geist, a 9-year-old fourth grader playing against a team heavy with fifth graders, was great in the paint, setting up shop in the lane to corral caroms and to go high in the sky to force the car cleansers' shots awry.

The Nets were picking them up at the city limits in a sticky man-to-man defense. Geist put the cuffs on the Washers' pivot man, sending him home empty in the scoring department.

Geist pilfered passes forced inside by the Washers, and his pocket-picking, along with that of Nets backcourt ace Mark Pennale, triggered the fast break. Pennale, a nifty ball-handler, scored four points and ran the Nets' potent offense. Nets forward Tyler Something-or-Other chipped in with four in shellacking the Car Washers.

The Auto Wash's cagers led only once in the game, 8–7 during the second quarter. But when the Washers' defense sagged to stop Geist in the lane, Tyler rang the bell from the baseline to put the Nets ahead to stay.

With Geist unstoppable, the score ballooned to 24–9 with two minutes remaining. It was time to collect the songbooks, and Tom, the Nets' coach, put Geist and Tyler on the pines.

Teams filing in for the second game were astonished to hear of young Geist's scoring feats and realized that the Nets, with their new tower of power, are a force to be reckoned with on the cage circuit. Almost as bad news for the other teams was that the Nets were playing without Offie, a talented forward, who will miss the first three games with finger complications.

Geist is handsome and excels in the classroom, and comparisons with U.S. senator Bill Bradley, former Rhodes scholar and basketball star of the local Princeton team and the New York Knicks, were inescapable. Geist's father, attractive mother, and cute sister were at the game.

Unusual at the Biddy level, an East Coast recruiter for Indiana University, whose son plays for the Nets, scouted Willie "Polter" Geist's debut. He liked what he saw.

∽

It's a lot of pressure on a fourth grader to have the Gray Lady covering his first game. Speaking of Bill Bradley, you'll recall, Dad, I dressed up as the former senator one year to ride a float in the Ridgewood Fourth of July parade. You and Mom said if I wanted to go as an athlete, it had to be him. Instead of Michael Jordan or L.T., I dressed as a long-retired, Princeton-educated Knick. There were confused stares from the other children.

By the time we hit sixth grade and the age of eleven, the level of competition in our local Biddy Basketball League got too tame, so we looked outside of town for games. The best players of our age got together and formed a traveling team that played the equivalent of an NBA schedule one season. No lie. We played in six different leagues and went 77–7. That's eighty-four games, two more than an NBA regular season slate. Our season was more grueling than the Knicks'. At least they were being paid.

We were coached at that point by the late great Bob Kossick, the larger-than-life father of my best friend and teammate, Mark. As you know, Dad, Bob was a tough, hard-charging, and totally lovable self-made man who had built New Jersey's National Community Bank from the ground up. As the bank's president and CEO he became something of a legend in the state of New Jersey. It was a legend our beloved Bob was happy to cultivate. The bank had bill-boards up across the state bearing the image of Bob's big, smiling face. If there was a message promoting bank business, no one noticed. All you saw was the giant floating head of Mark's dad, looming above the highways of the Garden State. Bob didn't do anything small. That included youth basketball.

Bob had us traversing northern New Jersey, playing in high school gyms, rec centers, and Catholic churches—all in the same day. A bunch of us would pile into Bob's Lincoln Town Car—always a Lincoln Town Car—and go wherever the schedule had us playing that Saturday. After finishing a game at St. Anne's Church in Fairlawn, New Jersey, we'd get in the car and Bob would dial the phone. This was back when it was a big deal to have a car phone. Bob always used speakerphone. His assistant Denise would answer the phone with directions to the next game, her voice crackling over the car phone connection and filling the air in the Lincoln: "Wyckoff is next." Off we went to Wyckoff. Then to Nutley. Then back to Mt. Carmel Church in Ridgewood for a home game. We did that eighty-four times that winter. Poor Denise spent her weekends as a basketball dispatcher.

We played for churches we didn't belong to ("Today you're Catholic") and against players who appeared to be middle-aged. We never quite knew where we were going next. Because no one could possibly carry enough uniforms for a day when we played six games, Bob conveniently drove around with a big cardboard box full of National Community Bank T-shirts in his trunk. In an emergency, when it wasn't clear whom we were supposed to be representing that game, we'd yank a bunch of NCB shirts out and play on, bonded by the opportunity for free bank advertising.

Our team, it must be said, was very good. As we laid waste to the competition in northern New Jersey, Bob thought it was time for a new challenge. One spring Saturday morning, you, Bob, and the other dads caravaned us out from Ridgewood to who-knows-where to play another game against God-knows-who. Maybe Wyckoff again. Maybe Glen Rock. But when we crossed the George Washington Bridge and then rolled up to the playground at 125th Street just off the FDR Drive in Harlem, it was clear we weren't in Wyckoff anymore. That's the playground with the famous "Crack is Wack" artwork on the handball wall. This was 1980s New York City. The one you covered every day for the *Times*. We were strictly representin' the 1980s suburbs. On went the National Community Bank T-shirts and out we were thrown to the wolves.

I don't recall that game being so much in a league as against a bunch of guys who were at the playground. I'll never forget the first possession, when our point guard Pete had the ball stolen from him by a shirtless man—it *was* a man—in a pair of blue jeans, who proceeded to go the length of the court for a vicious two-handed slam. He later left the game with his lovely wife and sweet children. Whoever those guys at 125th Street were, they blew us off the court and woke us up. They apparently didn't fear the boys from the 'burbs. Bob had given us a good lesson in humility, as only he could. His face smiled down at us from billboards all the way home. I sense you liked it too, Dad.

"The Debacle on 125th Street" proved to be good preparation for what awaited us the next year. Ridgewood High School was one of New Jersey's biggest public schools by enrollment. In both basketball and football, we left the leafy suburban leagues to meet new rivals in leafless places like Newark, Passaic, and Paterson. One of our very first ninth grade games came against Paterson's Eastside High, made infamous a couple of years prior in the movie *Lean On Me*. Morgan Freeman played Principal Joe Clark, the man who patrolled the hallways with a bullhorn and a baseball bat as he tried to clean up one of the country's most dangerous schools. Our principal, on the other hand, wore a maroon cardigan sweater and gave us high fives on the way to debate club. Security at Eastside was a little worried ahead of that first game about the new meat coming in from Ridgewood, so we got a police escort into the school. Guards lined the court during the game. It gave Eastside a decided home court advantage.

Once you got past the security state and the Paterson vagrants yelling at your school bus, though, the kids from Eastside turned out to be good guys. Many of them became friends and teammates on traveling teams outside of school. We lived together in hotel rooms on the road. During a national AAU tournament in the summer of 1991, we all went to see *Boyz n the Hood* in a packed Memphis movie theater. We got to know each other. As the years went on, the security guards seemed unnecessary. We knew these guys. We respected them. I'm not the type to get overly grandiose about the power of sports, but there isn't a whole lot I can think of beyond sports that has the power to make kids from the worst parts of Paterson and the best parts of Ridgewood feel they understand one another. My experience playing basketball and football changed the way I saw people whose lives I previously knew only from a scary movie about a principal with a baseball bat.

Life After Sports

Sports was a part of my life nearly every day until I got to college. We talked about it a lot, Dad, and I ultimately decided against playing small-college, Division III sports and went to Vanderbilt in Nashville. I had ideas about walking onto the football team. Then I saw the Alabama team get off the bus that first fall and headed straight for the bar instead. I became a sportswriter for the school paper—still close to the games, but with no threat of being mauled by an All-America linebacker from Florida or Georgia or Tennessee.

My final shred of collegiate athletic glory came at something called the Big Sky Basketball Tournament. *Glory* may be a strong word. It was a three-on-three backyard spectacle that included full contact (read: tackling), blackout drunk announcers, and a crowd that celebrated made baskets by raining beer cans and the occasional empty handle of Jack Daniel's onto the court. It essentially was a South American soccer match at a fraternity house in Nashville, Tennessee—without the riot police.

For all the trophies, state championships, and captaincies I accumulated over the years, I suspect you are most proud, Dad, of my Big Sky championship. In fact, when we were discussing this book, and a potential chapter about our sporting lives, you began with, "Well, you have to write about Big Sky, of course." So here you have it.

I had the distinct honor of playing in the championship game during my junior year. I'm able to remember every glorious moment because we the players were the only ones sober that night. The evening began, as all great sporting events do, with a tribute to America. A friend of mine actually rode a zip line from the roof of the house down to the court while playing "The Star-Spangled Banner" on a flaming guitar, as Roman candles fired from his instrument. He was shirtless and wearing an army helmet. After he played the final patriotic note, my friend smashed his guitar on the court, Pete Townshend style, as fireworks continued to shoot in every direction toward the crowd. It was terrifying and spectacular. It remains one of the wildest things I've ever witnessed in person.

As the pregame festivities continued, Miss Big Sky made an appearance at midcourt to dramatically pull a velvet shroud off the tournament's freshly painted logo. I'm happy to say I married Miss Big Sky 1997. No one can take that away from me.

Next, it was time to meet the "mystery dunker"—perhaps

the most anticipated moment of the evening. The man's identity was known beforehand only to the tournament commissioner. The mystery dunker's job was to conceal his identity with a mask or disguise, but to be just about nude everywhere else, save for a jockstrap or loincloth. The mystery dunker bolted from the house just before tip-off, threw down a dunk, and then scampered away into the night. I may or may not have been the mystery dunker one year. I may or may not have worn greasepaint and a fright wig and dropped a tomahawk dunk to the cheers (i.e., thrown beer cans) of the crowd.

The game itself was secondary to the show, and that was reflected in the piss-poor scorekeeping. The commissioner was responsible for keeping tabs on the score, but he generally was not in a state to perform even elementary mathematics. During our championship game, the commish botched the score time and again before retiring to the front bushes to nap for the remainder of the evening. As with the USA/USSR gold medal game at the 1972 Olympics in Munich, there remains to this day dispute about who really won Big Sky that year. All I know is, my name is on the plaque.

Another of your favorite moments from my sports career came during my brief attempt to play the Beautiful Game as a kid. I was never any good at soccer. Not enough pushing or tackling. You laughed from the sideline during a youth soccer game as I did the only thing I was good at on a soccer field: taunting my opponent. I stood across the midfield line from my friend Eric before a kickoff and he and I challenged each other as if we were professional wrestlers.

Hulk Hogan was our hero at the time and he did a thing where he'd point at his opponent, smack his hands together three times to symbolize the three-count he would get as he pinned the meek challenger, and then make a big gesture in front of his waist as if putting on an imaginary championship belt after the victory. It's a move since stolen by Packers quarterback Aaron Rodgers for use after he scores a touchdown. It's no wonder soccer and I never really clicked—I was too busy making wrestling taunts to actually understand the rules of the game. And really, what's with the no-hands thing?

You and I spent long hours over the years playing catch in the backyard, taking batting practice at the middle school down the street, and shooting three-pointers in the driveway you'd had shaped explicitly around the basketball hoop. Once in a while, these days, we'll pick up the little gloves I bought for the kids and throw the baseball around with them. Six-year-old Lucie's got a good little arm on her. Four-year-old George is still trying to figure out whether he's a righty or a lefty. We're pushing him to the left hand so he can achieve his (our) boyhood dream of becoming a grossly overpaid left-handed spot reliever in the big leagues one day, and caring for the needs of his father.

Sports for us, I think it's fair to say, Dad, are now pretty much about spectating and debating. We bond over the Yankees, the Knicks, the Illini, and the Southeastern Conference's newest football powerhouse, the Vanderbilt Commodores (#AnchorDown), and we've begun to come to terms with the *possibility* that neither of us will play third base for the Yankees or point guard for the Knicks. So instead we get together and judge the people who occupy those positions now.

We do get out and hack around the public nine-hole golf course on Shelter Island sometimes. It's a fabulous little place called Goat Hill. The gray, shingled clubhouse sits up on a hill overlooking Dering Harbor, dotted with sailboats. The wraparound porch is covered in fencing to protect diners from the reliably errant tee shots that serve as incoming fire from the ninth tee every few minutes. I'm proud to say I once drilled the broadside of a passing beer truck off the tee and the ball ricocheted back into play, where I got up and down for par. That's Goat Hill.

Inside the clubhouse we sit at the bar with locals who don't necessarily come for the golf. It's just a good place to have a Budweiser in a bottle and roll a bunch of dice out of a cup for a shot at the pot of money behind the bar. Someone sitting down at the bar might say, "Beer and a roll, please." He's not asking for a dinner roll. He wants a beer and the cup with the dice. If he hits a certain combination, he wins the pot. Two bucks a roll. That's Goat Hill.

The course itself will never be mistaken for Augusta National. But then you and I never have been Augusta National material, either on the course or inside the men's grill. We've never belonged to a club in our lives, unless you count the Shelter Island VFW hall with a bowling alley in the basement. All the Little League, the eighty-four-game middle school basketball seasons, and the high school games against Eastside are behind us now. You and I are happy being the kind of "athletes" who cruise around Goat Hill searching in vain for our golf balls while bitching about A-Rod. That's fun too.

Coach Bill on Sports

You were eleven, Willie, when we bought that dilapidated century-old Victorian house that required complete refurbishing inside and out, floors to ceilings, kitchen, bathrooms, porches, everything. Where to begin? We had to prioritize. So we started the massive renovation by cutting down a big tree in the backyard and putting in a basketball court, curved to allow three-point shots. Floors for the house—nonexistent in various places—would have to wait.

You became a good player, started on the varsity as a sophomore, and by God you could hit the three. At six-four you could dunk. I really didn't care if you accomplished anything else in life and told you so.

I was one of the most, if not the most, vociferous (read: obnoxious) fans at your basketball games, shouting at the referees when they made "bad calls" that favored the opposition: "Stick around for the team picture, ref!" Stuff like that, which without question would have embarrassed any son, but you never complained. Sorry, Will.

But these Easterners had no concept of how important high school basketball was. When our local girls' team won the state tournament—*the state tournament!*—there was little mention of it. Jody and I took it upon ourselves to make a congratulatory billboard and put it up on the railroad underpass in the center of town.

I've loved basketball from my days growing up in Illinois, from nights when my dad volunteered to man a side door (for coaches and officials only) at high school games and took me along from the time I was about five. Few people outside Midwestern small towns can relate to this scene. The thousand-or-so-seat gym, bleachers and balcony, were packed on Friday nights. Our cheerleaders were whipping the crowd into a frenzy. On a stage at one end of the gym a loud twenty-five-member band belted out fight songs as the players, in their flashy satiny warm-up suits, glided through pregame layup drills. It was intense. When our Champaign Maroons played the hated Urbana Tigers it was mayhem. I recall a home game when the Tigers' gangly six-foot-eight center named Shoemaker was introduced and our fans threw dozens of shoes onto the court.

When you became a young basketball star, I dreamed of moving to a small town in Indiana for your high school years so you could be properly idolized by the guys down at the coffee shop, who'd tell their good-for-nothing sons to be more like you and their daughters to reward your achievements, each in her own way.

You were co-captain your senior year of both the basketball and football teams. I never made those teams. More than once I was the last guy cut. One year it was because F. M. Walker jumped over me on his way to the hoop during tryouts. I can remember walking down the long hallway toward the list posted on the locker room door of those who'd made the basketball team, hoping and praying, to no avail. If that sounds heartbreaking, good.

Football was a stretch. I was a skinny kid, and when called upon to tackle a big rumbling fullback I'd find myself rolling backward in a heap of equipment: helmet and shoulder pads. I was good at baseball until they started throwing looping curveballs. And until I found myself "playing" (in a broad sense) the same position as the coach's son.

Back when you were getting involved in sports lacrosse was still this weird new basket-on-a-stick activity neither of us could relate to. Soccer? Un-American. I had tried wrestling, briefly. Twiggy and nearly six feet tall, I was melted down by coaches to the 120-pound weight class. Starved and steamed, I was a ramen noodle when it was time to take the mat and do battle against stronger, faster little Schwarzeneggers. If I had been a member of the Donner Party, I would have been an appetizer.

So I lettered in cross-country. Ever try to get laid with a cross-country letter?

⌒∽

My father did nothing to encourage me athletically. He played the piano, not catch. But there were plenty of kids on our block (every block in the US, in those days) and we played baseball games most every summer night in our backyard. My mother bowed her head in prayer before each game, asking protection for our picture window, which was just down the third base line, for the sapling she had planted all too near second base, and for the neighbors' new Buick, parked in their driveway in left field.

I took you, Willie, on the El train to Chicago Cubs games, where you devoured hot dogs and ice cream but seemed generally uninterested in the game itself, which is actually the only approach to enjoying a Cubs game. You were too young to get drunk.

As you said, when we moved to New York you quickly

took to the Yankees. There was always great drama in the clubhouse, they were on TV every night, and they won. I'd told you in Chicago that there really were no winners or losers, but you were learning otherwise, watching ticker tape parades for world champion Yankees teams in New York's Canyon of Heroes.

Remember when you and I met a scalper at a designated parking space at the Mets' stadium and paid him a year's salary for two tickets to a Yankees–Mets subway series in 2000? I pretended to be for the Mets (I'm a National League, St. Louis Cardinals fan by birth) and acted disappointed when they lost four games to one. And yes, we were both Mets fans at the '86 World Series games.

Before Little League, you would play ball by yourself in the backyard, singing the national anthem, doing the announcing, hitting an imaginary ball, running the bases, and sliding into home. Safe! Most often you would hit home runs. I'd done the same sort of thing at my grandparents' house in the St. Louis area, where my dad, a high school teacher, worked summers for a newspaper. I'd pitch to a tree, then field the ball and throw it to the side of the house, until my grandmother told me to stop.

Soon enough there you were, Willie, standing in your uniform, complete with matching wristbands, taking practice swings as you awaited your first at-bat ever. I realized that this was the first time in your life you faced true adversaries, cutthroat competitors trying to make you fail, get you out. Nine of the little bastards. It didn't seem fair.

Make that ten. The umpire called the first pitch a strike, even though it was over your head. I groaned and glanced at Jody, who was giving the man a menacing "kill the umpire" glare. It wasn't rhetorical; she wanted—in fact, she had the biological imperative—to actually kill him to protect her young.

The next pitch was even higher, so high the ump had no choice but to call it a ball or else. The next pitch rolled over the plate. "Ball two." Hey, maybe our son would get a walk. A free pass. A walk sounded just fine, a pleasant stroll to first, where he'd be *safe*. Safe from all these jackals. You wanted a hit. You expected to get a hit every time, as in the backyard, and didn't understand that three hits in ten at-bats by those Yankees you saw on TV made them very rich indeed.

I knew you were going to swing at the next one no matter where it was. You did and there was a "plink" as the ball met the aluminum bat. The ball was headed toward the gap between the first and second basemen, but slowly. Very slowly. Surely the second baseman would get to it, eventually. But no. You stood at the plate, watching the ball.

"Run, Willie!" I shouted.

"Run! Run! Run!" Jody screamed.

And you began to run.

We have a definite sports bond. We've gone together to several World Series games, two Final Four weekends, and the Rose and Sugar Bowls, and, of course, have enjoyed some unusual events: WrestleMania I, for example, where Liberace was the timekeeper and Muhammad Ali a guest referee.

On another occasion we sat in Donald Trump's box with The Donald, watching his short-lived New Jersey Generals of the short-lived USFL, with the legendary Howard Cosell drinking dark-brown cocktails and calling the game for just us. Surreal.

For better or worse, sports are probably still the basis of and starting point for most of our conversations (not counting photons, quarks, and wave-particle duality). But I qualify this because your children seem to be surpassing sports as a topic of discussion. George and Lucie are the best and lately the Yankees, Mets, Knicks, Nets, Jets, Rangers, Islanders, and Illini haven't provided much you'd really talk about.

My granddaughter, Lucie, six, swims like a fish, and grandson George, four, swims too, albeit at the Tadpole level, which is just a notch above Drowning. I didn't swim until I was…what? Nineteen? No, but it was fifth or sixth grade. My mom would drop me off at the YMCA for lessons and Ricky Piper and I would ditch out and walk downtown. Who knows why? On the way back, we'd stop at the West Side Park fountain and wet our towels before Mom picked us up at the Y.

Swimming was *really* weird back then, let me tell ya. Boys swam nude, completely naked at the Y! Why doesn't that surprise me? The stated reasons for this policy were the impracticality of providing and maintaining sanitary swimsuits and the need to keep lint fibers from the suits from clogging the filtration system. Sure. And get this! Mandatory swim classes for boys at Edison Junior High School were also conducted in the nude! Way awkward. It's a wonder any of us ever went near a pool again.

Ice skating was big in my hometown, the local rink producing a number of world-class skaters (Bonnie Blair, Katherine Reutter, et al) but I gave it up after some idiot ran over my thumb with his blade. No skiing. The steepest slope in my hometown was our driveway; there were no mountains for about a thousand miles in any direction. We took you and Libby once to Vermont, where we tried to learn to ski in the rain. Fun. No tennis or golf, those were for the clubby set, not us.

I played tennis once with an old racket that had belonged to an uncle killed in World War II, but the first time I swung at a ball it went straight through the strings. Game, set, match.

Our family did play a lot of mini golf, as does yours, and once a year or so the two of us try the real thing. We'd arrive at a public course, rent some awful clubs that looked like fireplace tools (a few with screws coming out of the bottoms of the drivers), and all of them six to twelve inches too short for you. The first tee was always the worst, because inevitably there would be people waiting to tee off...and watching. We were very courteous about insisting they go before us, and once it was our turn we'd hurry our shots before others arrived.

It takes a lot of balls for us to play golf (pun not intended, just unavoidable). You're a big guy and can hit the ball as far as some pros, just not in any particular direction. I often hit the ball roughly as far as a croquet player. Often I hit a house across the street from the second fairway on the Shelter Island course, but the owner just laughs as he points out the holes in his house and sells the golf balls three for a dollar. You and I laugh and swear a lot out on the links. You used to throw your clubs. You did this in a very deliberate way, pausing a second or two to let your anger dissipate, then letting fly. You had style.

You also like to call the action when we play, impersonating a golf announcer like, say, Jim Nantz. Speaking softly, like Jim, you'll break into "Striding up the final fairway approaching the eighteenth green here at historic (nine-hole) Shelter Island Country Club, walking in the footsteps of Palmer, Nicklaus, and Snead, applause breaks out for these two champions."

Meanwhile my tee shot will have bounced high off a side street and ended up either in the front yard of that ranch home or on the porch. Porch shots are tough. They can prompt 911 calls, and hitting out of all that porch furniture is tricky. It is not immediately clear where your tee shot is right now, perhaps on an adjacent fairway. But we use your mom's rule: Play the closest hole.

I like to think that for all our love of sports, we kept them in the proper perspective. After your last high school football game, a defeat on our home field in a state championship semifinal game, you took off your helmet and trotted the length of the field alone, ending up in the end zone where the previous season you had scored the only touchdown to win the state championship. You were soaking it all in. This was your last football game ever. You loved the game. You loved being on this team. You were saying goodbye to all that. Fans walked onto the field and I did something inappropriate for a football dad. I kissed you on the cheek.

I have always looked askance at parents who feel the need to make claims that a youth sport is much more than a game, that it builds character eight ways (or is that Wheaties?), makes men and women out of boys and girls, keeps them off crack cocaine, and provides a healthy alternative to carjacking and robbing 7-Elevens. What's wrong with being just a game?

But I have to admit, I do believe you learned some valuable lessons from football and basketball, some things I had to learn fast in the military, first and foremost dependability and responsibility. As well as loyalty, determination, strength, and at times even courage.

Recently you confided in me that instead of encouraging you in sports I should have had you take guitar lessons, so that you would now be a rich and famous rock star. "Money for nuthin', chicks for free" and all that. (I can just picture Mrs. Hendrix dropping off little Jimi at guitar lessons.) That would have been good to know before we felled a mighty oak and paved the backyard to make a basketball court, Willie.

Geist Date in History

October 3, 1989

Willie's great-grandfather on Jody's side, Herbie Lewis, is inducted into the Hockey Hall of Fame during a ceremony in Toronto. Bobby, as he was known in the family, was one of the game's all-time greats, captaining the Detroit Red Wings in the 1930s and leading them to back-to-back Stanley Cup titles in 1936 and 1937. Curiously, given his pedigree, Willie spends most of his brief youth skating career barreling completely out of control into small children while wearing a rented pair of figure skates.

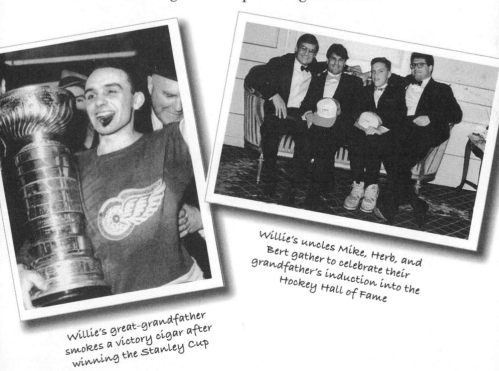

Willie's uncles Mike, Herb, and Bert gather to celebrate their grandfather's induction into the Hockey Hall of Fame

Willie's great-grandfather smokes a victory cigar after winning the Stanley Cup

Chapter 8

A Four-Year-Old, a Football Game & Dora the Explorer

WILLIE

In the fall of 2011, I took my then four-year-old daughter, Lucie, to her first football game: Columbia hosting Harvard in

Lucie, four, off to either preschool or Hollywood

Lucie, age four

*a late-season Ivy League clash of the academic titans. I wrote
about the day in a piece published on Grantland.com.*

How to Take Your Four-Year-Old Daughter
to a Football Game

When you live in New York City, you run up a long
list of things you've been meaning to do. You've been
meaning to get to some off-Broadway theater—your
trip to see Blue Man Group with relatives in from
Schaumburg doesn't count. You've been meaning to
get out to Ellis Island, which you hear has a data-
base that allows you to track the immigrant history
of your family. That sounds cool. You've been meaning to dust off the tuxedo and see *Don Giovanni* at
the Met. You'll probably have some champagne and
light hors d'oeuvres while you're there. And you've
been meaning to get over to Brooklyn to see what
all the fuss is about. Maybe pick up a porkpie hat
and some skinny ties or something.

But you don't do these things. You will drive by
the places where these things could happen very
easily and you will be reminded that you've been
meaning to do them. You can't really explain why
you haven't done them. You'd like to think it's
because you're so busy, but you somehow keep finding time to do things every weekend like watch that
noon, Saturday ESPN2 game between Northwestern
and Iowa, with the winner remaining right in the
thick of the TicketCity Bowl conversation.

High on the list of things I've been meaning to
do since I moved to New York in 2004 is going up

to a Columbia University football game. I blame myself for the failure to make this happen for seven years, but I will say it's tough to find a wingman for a trip like that, and a solo mission to watch an Ivy League school with which I have absolutely no affiliation always felt like a bridge I didn't want to cross. I also struggled, when raising the idea every year, to answer my wife's fundamental question, "Why the hell am I going to sit in the cold to watch a football game between Columbia and Brown?" This year, I stopped asking my wife. Instead, I found a wingman who does not ask the kind of questions that reduce a man's long-held dreams to trivia. I invited my helpless four-year-old daughter.

Granted, my sales pitch was vague. I told Lucie we were going on a "subway adventure." That could have meant we were going to the Museum of Natural History, where she's on a first-name basis with the life-size elephants and runs a tab at the gift shop. It could have meant we were going to live out some wild four-year-old fantasy, like swimming in a pool full of Jolly Ranchers while Angelina Ballerina and Handy Manny cheered us on. Or it could have meant we were going to watch the winless Columbia Lions play host to Harvard at Lawrence A. Wien Stadium. Luckily, she didn't ask for details.

Lucie was a great date. She enthusiastically packed the giant pink Dora the Explorer backpack that consumes three-quarters of her body with two apples, some Goldfish crackers, a scarf, and a hat. I threw in some toys on the off chance the Ivy League football game somehow didn't hold her attention. My wife was happy to see the two of us off, mainly because she knew that after seven years of kicking the can down the road, she was off the hook forever. She stayed home with our two-year-old son, whose naptime didn't jibe with the twelve thirty p.m. kickoff. Come to think of it, he may have been faking a nap so he didn't have to come to the game.

Lucie and I stepped out of our apartment building into the chilly afternoon (game-time temperature was forty-five degrees) and hopped on the 1 train. When you get on the subway to go to a Yankees game, you know you're on the right train. Everyone is in jerseys, drinking, and talking loudly about how A. J. Burnett sucks. The subway to the Columbia game is different. And by "different," I mean "empty." For twelve stops and about twenty minutes, it was just me, Lucie, and a shoeless, sleeping gentleman who I suspect was not headed up to the Columbia alumni tailgate. Might have been a Harvard man.

By the time we got off the subway at the 215th Street station—the last in Manhattan before you cross over into the Bronx—you finally could tell there was something going on. A small crowd was marching up the hill on 218th Street. We followed the trail of powder blue and white balloons that signaled either a college football game or a five-year-old boy's birthday party.

At the gate, guards dressed in the familiar yellow "Event Security" windbreakers asked to take a peek inside Lucie's Dora backpack. This seemed excessive on a number of levels. If Al-Qaeda was targeting sparsely attended Ivy League football games, it was news to me, and a little pathetic if you don't mind my saying so. And I know jihadists have been on the ropes lately, but are they really using Scandinavian-looking New York City preschoolers to carry out their missions? If so, shame on them. Luckily, the Honeycrisp apples checked out, and we walked up to the ticket booth, Lucie slid a crisp twenty-dollar bill through the window, and back came two light-blue tickets that would announce forever, on the front of a refrigerator and probably later in the bottom of a shoe box, that I had been to a Columbia football game on November 5, 2011. I officially was doing the thing I'd been meaning to do. I was unreasonably excited to be there.

Lucie set the tone for the day when she asked almost immediately after we sat down on our cold, metal bleacher seats, "How long do we have to stay here?" It was time for some quick appeasement.

"They have hot chocolate," I said.

"Where?!" she shot back.

"They sell it at halftime," I told her, but she wanted more.

"Do they have Swedish red fish at this football game?" she asked.

"I bet they do," I replied. Satisfied for the moment, she settled into her seat. I had just bought myself two quarters of football with the promise of a halftime sugar buy.

I guess I hadn't considered beforehand how entertaining it would be to have a four-year-old little girl breaking down the game at my side as she ate Goldfish and pounded juice boxes. Columbia was wearing its home blue jerseys. Harvard was in white with shiny gold pants. Lucie quickly dubbed this a battle between "The Golden Pants" and "The Light-Blue Shirt Guys." For the record, I will call Harvard "The Golden Pants" for the rest of my life.

I told Lucie we were rooting for Columbia because they're the New York team (she's too young for me to explain that no one roots for Harvard in anything—in sports or in life). But she didn't care what I told her about Columbia: She was blinded by "The Golden Pants." That was her team. Those were her pants. After every play—and I mean *every* play—she asked if "The Golden Pants" had won the game. At this rate, it was going to be a long day. Everything changed, though, on a fateful pass-interference call in the second quarter.

Columbia threw a deep ball over the middle. The defensive back gave a little shove, the receiver went down, the flags flew, and the home crowd (the reported 4,153 seemed about right) booed, then cheered loudly. Lucie asked me what had happened.

I told her the "Golden Pants" guy pushed down the "Light-Blue Shirt Guy" and broke the rules. She whipped her head around, mimicking the stern look her mother gives her when she's caught smacking her little brother around.

"He pushed him?" she asked. She was ready to call The Hague.

"Yes," I said. "And that's against the rules."

Lucie glared at the field, and with pursed lips repeated a line she herself had heard many times before in her own home: "We *do not* push." You have never seen someone switch a sports allegiance so quickly. Suddenly, she was a dyed-in-the-wool Columbia fan, if such a thing exists. The pass interference was more than a penalty. It was a violation. A moral failing. Grounds for a time-out at her preschool, so why not here at Lawrence A. Wien Stadium? How, pray tell, would a little yellow flag deter that kind of behavior in the future? It was a scandal. Lucie had placed her trust in that Harvard team some thirty-two minutes earlier, and now, as far as she was concerned, it was over. Lucie didn't even know "The Golden Pants" anymore.

Now she at least was rooting for the right team, but another problem arose: the lion at the game. Not the Columbia mascot—Lucie picked up right away that he was not a real lion and therefore not a threat. No, it was a sound coming from the loudspeakers on the scoreboard behind the north end zone over and over again. A loud, prolonged lion's roar. Lucie covered her ears in horror and turned to me with a stunning revelation.

"Daddy," she said ominously. "There's a lion at this football game."

I assured her there were no real lions at the game, but she had her doubts. She'd heard her share of lion roars on the iPad Animal Sounds app over the years, and this one sounded like the real thing. And, by the way, there were pictures of lions everywhere. There on the press box: a lion. There in the program: a lion. There on that lady's sweatshirt: another lion! They named the team after lions, for Christ's sake! The way Lucie saw it, it was only a matter of time before this lion burst onto the field and ate all the "Golden Pants" and "Light-Blue Shirt Guys." Lucie, not unreasonably from her point of view, wanted out of Lawrence A. Wien Stadium before we all were mauled. My long-deferred romantic dream of watching Columbia football under the autumn sun was in serious jeopardy. It was about that time that, as if sent from the heavens, a seagull swooped down and shit on my head.

There had been a good-size flock of seagulls hovering over the stadium all afternoon, scattering away from punts and returning to mill around the large sections of unpopulated bleachers. One of these little bastards locked in on me and dropped one right on top of my dome.

Not great for Dad, but really, really great for four-year-old daughter. My horror turned to relief. One

laugh-out-loud, laser-guided seagull bomb completely neutralized the threat of the man-eating lion
living in the scoreboard. That act of unintentional
physical comedy and the halftime hot chocolate
and candy (FYI, they do not have Swedish Fish at
the Lawrence A. Wien Stadium concession stands)
bought my way into the third quarter, but I knew
my time was short. The M&M's would wear off soon,
and jacked-up Lucie would eventually stop running
the stadium stairs like she was Walter Payton in an
off-season training session. Plus my daughter, at
the tender age of four, had already figured out the
difficult lesson that non-sporting girlfriends and
wives eventually learn: Sports Time is a lie. The
scoreboard said there were seven minutes left in
the third quarter, so when she asked, "How much
longer, Dad?" I lied and told her seven minutes. We
all know Sports Time equals Time on Clock times
three (ST = TOCx3). Now my daughter knows that,
too. I tried it on her later in the quarter, and she
called me out immediately: "Daddy, this is *not* three
minutes! Did you forget I want to go home?"

After a tight first half, Columbia started to play
like the 0–7 team it was, and Harvard, leading the
Ivy League, remembered it was Harvard—the school
that produced the Unabomber. (Note: If you are a
Harvard admissions director reading this in some
far-flung corner of the Internet thirteen years from
now, don't hold it against Lucie. It's her dad's fault.)
A forty-one-yard touchdown pass from Collier

Winters made it 28–14 in the third quarter, and Lucie was begging out: "The Golden Pants keep winning. Let's go!"

I stretched our day into the fourth quarter by letting Lucie draw in the game program—she colored in the head shot of Columbia University president Lee Bollinger. I did what I had to do. But when Harvard's Kyle Juszczyk hauled in a pass, broke two tackles, and dove into the end zone for another long touchdown, the score was 35–14 and we were done. "The Golden Pants" had the game wrapped up, the scoreboard lion was quiet, and there was the very real threat that another one of these goddamned seagulls was going to paint me up again. It was time to go.

We walked out of the stadium, past a Muslim fan who had stepped outside to pray (I'm guessing you didn't see that at the LSU-Alabama game that same day in Tuscaloosa), and up the steps to the subway station. The 1 train was a lot more crowded going south to the city late on a Saturday afternoon than it had been going north to the Columbia game three hours earlier. Lucie, with her Dora backpack strapped on and her giant blue No. 1 finger on her hand, put her head in my lap and fell asleep. Seven long years to do just one of the things I'd been meaning to do in New York and, at that moment, well worth the wait. Thank you, "Light-Blue Shirt Guys."

Postscript

Shortly after that piece was published on Grantland, I received a letter from the dean of undergraduate admissions at Harvard. Official Harvard letterhead and everything. The dean wrote that Lucie's initial instinct to root for the right team was an impressive one and that my four-year-old daughter had been placed on Harvard's list of "Ones to Watch." It was a great, unexpected response from the school—almost enough to make me root for Harvard. *Almost.*

Geist Date in History
March 31, 1985

On assignment as a *New York Times* columnist, Bill covers the World Wrestling Federation's very first WrestleMania at Madison Square Garden. While Bill works his sources (or something), nine-year-old Willie and his mom, Jody, have prime seats for the festivities. The man seated next to Willie and Jody pulls up his pant leg to reveal a knife in his boot, which he says he'll use if anyone "messes with the Hulkster." No one, as it turns out, messes with Hulk Hogan to an extent that calls for a citizen's knife-wielding intervention. Willie, a little Hulkamaniac himself, gets to meet Hogan backstage. It's like meeting Santa Claus and getting the proof of what you've known all along: He's real.

Libby admires Willie, doing his best Hulk Hogan pose

Chapter 9

Talking to Teens About Drinking (Once They've Reached Their Thirties)

BILL

I'm told there really are parents who actually believe they have the power to stop their teenagers from drinking. Seriously.

Fine. Let them lock down their children so that the wee ones' lips never touch a can of Budweiser or a bottle of Carlo Rossi. These are the parents who are shocked when their kid's meth lab in the garage blows sky-high.

Willie's best man, Mark, and friends raise their glasses at Christina and Willie's wedding

Why do they want to stop teenagers' drinking? Look at Europe. Wait. OK, look at Monaco, Luxembourg, or Liechtenstein. In many countries, parents serve their children wine with meals. (Unsure which vintage best accompanies Gerber strained peas and carrots.)

The point being: As those kids grow up they develop an appreciation of wine and other alcoholic beverages as something more than mind-numbing drugs capable of producing medically induced comas. They also learn their capacities for tolerance in the presence of their own families, their beds but steps away. In Wisconsin, where my daughter attended college, the drinking age was twenty-one, but I could legally buy her a beer (or, presumably, a martini) when she was eighteen (maybe even when she was ten) because she was with a parent.

As for you, Willie, I'm not sure when you had your first beer. Boy Scouts?

For me, it started while I was working summers at my uncle's resort at Lake of the Ozarks in Missouri. As a high school sophomore, I'd try to party with the staff of experienced collegiate drinkers and would find myself, yes, heaving in the bushes or driving the porcelain bus. Eventually I invented a method for staying sober a bit longer, which I believe I've shared with you. I called it the "Butt and Crack" method: A half hour before consuming alcoholic beverages, drink a twelve-ounce glass of whole milk while eating fifteen saltine crackers slathered with butter. The science behind this is simple, really: coating the stomach wall to reduce the alcohol absorption rate. Great in the lab, but field tests failed to achieve positive results.

My uncle, a functioning alcoholic, counseled me: "Drink Scotch and water and you won't get sick." It was one of

Uncle Ed's tips for teens. That fall I was the only sixteen-year-old in town who drank Scotch.

As in all things, Will, you were discreet about drinking. I first saw you quaff a beer when you were a senior in high school. You chugged a stein in our kitchen in a manner that suggested it was not your first.

My view is that parents who forbid their seventeen-year-olds a beer are revealing to their children how totally out of it they are. If kids are allowed a supervised drink here and there, when it comes time to instruct them "Absolutely no drinking and driving," they'll know it's coming from a reasonable source.

We were those parents you read about in the tabloids who have been brought up on criminal charges for "knowingly allowing" underage drinking in their homes. Not a lot. A couple of times.

In your senior year of high school, Willie, word of a party at the Geists' spread like wildfire, and way before "social media." If you invited ten, you could expect ten squared. You knew this equation, so you designated the largest of your football teammates as bouncers, turning away some unknowns and riding herd on those who looked as if they might be on the verge of inflicting property damage. Still, one guest fell through the porch railing (my bad) as the crowd exploded to ten-squared-plus.

To no one's surprise, the gendarmes arrived. I met them in the driveway and preemptively offered to turn down the volume on the blasting rap.

"No," said one of the officers, "the complaint we received was about the noise of that bus idling beneath your neighbor's bedroom window."

"Bus?!"

People were arriving by bus for the party at Geists' house. I didn't check for out-of-state plates.

Not all the parties were "knowingly allowed." There was that time Jody and I returned from a weekend away and would not have even known there had been a sizable social function in our home had it not been for the seven coolers stacked neatly on the side porch. Spic-and-span. Truly an amazing job, Will. You were clearly ready for cleaning up Superfund hazardous waste sites.

When the party wasn't at our house, you had a prime alternative venue. As you've said, your best buddy Mark had a big bedroom suite on the third floor of his home and his father, Bob, hung out on the second floor, in part to inter-dict party supplies (e.g., beer and girls) on the stairway to heaven. Bob was a force to be reckoned with. One night he phoned me and said, "You won't believe what's going on over here. There are ninjas going up the side of my house!" Our kids were taught rock climbing in their gym classes and were using their newfound skills to ascend with ropes the side of Bob's house on their way to the summit—the third floor. Cases of beer were hoisted on pulleys. I can't recall if girls were climbing too, but Bob did discover a couple of them in Mark's closet. Would that trigonometry proved as valuable a class as rock climbing.

Willie's (Underage) Toast to Dad

As a seventeen-year-old, I certainly endorsed and appreci-ated your liberal stance on underage drinking, Dad. I'm not sure most high school seniors have a boilermaker with dinner after football practice, but it worked for us. I've handled booze responsibly all my life, with some exceptions, of course. I'm willing to give your progressive parenting methods credit for that. And sorry again about the charter buses idling outside the house. In hindsight, busing in guests from across the Tri-State area for a basement party may have been excessive. Lucrative (we charged admission), but excessive.

We did pretty well with beer in those days once we had it, but *securing* it was fraught with risk, danger, and a little crime. Hanging around the parking lot of the 7-Eleven asking strangers to buy us beer was not a good look, so we developed a sophisticated process of making fake IDs. And it all took place in your lovely eat-in kitchen.

Here's how it worked: We started with an original New Jersey state driver's license belonging to a seventeen-year-old born in, say, 1975. We'd bring one of Mom's pots to a boil on the stove top while she started the fettuccine on another burner. Once we had a nice steam working, we'd hold the license over the pot and allow the glue on the laminate to loosen. After a minute or so, we could peel the plastic cover off the license, exposing the print below—license number, name, address, and, most importantly, date of birth.

Next came a custom Wite-Out, mixed to match the color of the background on the Jersey license. Like a skilled surgeon, one of us would place a tiny, smooth dab over only the *5* in *1975*, leaving *197* followed by a blank white space. Now, before we began this kitchen process, we'd used a computer to print out, on clear plastic, exact replicas of the license—showing the same printed information from the original, except with the year of birth changed to 1970.

When the Wite-Out was dry we laid the new plastic sheet over the old license. The text lined up and covered every other character perfectly, and the *1970* fell over the old *1975*, with the Wite-Out hiding any trace of that old *5* beneath. Then we'd use one of our moms' irons—in this case *my* mom's—to seal the new laminate. Just like that, I aged five years in the eyes of the state of New Jersey. I was a twenty-two-year-old high school junior.

I'll never forget the time a group of us went into one restaurant whose bar we had frequented throughout high school and college to celebrate a friend's actual twenty-first birthday. "Twenty-first birthday?!" our stunned regular bartender asked. "You guys have been coming in here for five years!" We also occasionally used to go in high school to another place just over Route 17 for burgers and a pitcher of beer during lunch break. It made the second half of a long school day much more festive.

My good friend who was the mastermind behind the criminal syndicate made some nice walking-around money for a high school kid. Just imagine if we'd spent all that time and ingenuity thinking up Facebook instead of making fake IDs.

That's not to say the IDs were foolproof. One of the great stories in Geist lore took place as a result of those fake IDs. I need not remind you of this one, Dad. Mark and I were with you, Mom, and Libby on vacation in Nantucket the summer before we went off to college. We'd been drinking casually in bars for so long that we strolled up to one confidently expecting to breeze in as usual. The bouncer, though, was not impressed with our forgery. He tugged at our licenses, called them fakes, and told us to stand right where we were. The police station was right across the street—literally ten steps away. I didn't say we were smart.

The bouncer got the cops involved and my dear old friend Mark decided to make a run for it. Before I knew what had happened, I'd been apprehended by Nantucket's finest. Mark, a star football running back, dashed off into the night. Dad, you were kind to come on down to the station to bail me out, but what they really wanted was the fugitive. On that night, Mark was Jason Bourne, eluding authorities by changing his dress, thumbing rides with strangers, and jumping over privet hedges as he moved through backyards. *The Bourne Fake Identity.* Finally, after we'd returned home, the phone rang in our rental cottage. It was Mark. He was safe, but he couldn't talk long—they were probably listening.

Dad, you eventually convinced Mark to come back home and we turned ourselves in. You masterfully talked us out of arrests and court dates that would have brought us back to the island from college. In exchange, though, we were sentenced to "rehab" for the remainder of our stay—about a week. Fake ID rehab, I guess it was.

The poor therapist who treated us at the hospital annex where we served our sentence tried to make it a real thing. She really did, God bless her. She had impressive medical degrees on the wall of her office and a nice way about her, but she learned after about five minutes that we weren't addicts. Idiots, yes. Addicts, no. Our "rehab" therapist moved on quickly from chemical dependence to STDs to eating disorders to rare avian diseases. We went through the whole textbook. We had none of these conditions, but

we listened respectfully. We also posed for pictures to com-
memorate our stint in the joint. By way of thanks, she gave
us glow-in-the-dark condoms and told us to stay safe. We
had been rehabilitated. Sorry we didn't see more of you
and Mom on that trip, Dad.

Another drinking night for which I'd like to take this
opportunity to apologize is the one at the Dory. Need I say
more? The Dory is a great little bar on Shelter Island, New
York. We've been going there for nearly twenty years. We
still go a few times a summer. We had Libby's rehearsal
dinner there. One summer about a dozen or so years ago,
I brought a group of my college friends from Vanderbilt
out for the weekend. After dinner we went to the Dory for
drinks. It was hopping, as it usually is on a Saturday night,
filled mostly with locals. I was proud to show my buddies
around the island we love.

There was no mistaking as we walked in that my crew
was not from around those parts. You know, more light
summer sweaters and soft-leather loafers in our group than
in the rest of the crowd. When we walked through the
front door of the Dory that night, we got everything but
the record scratch and the Old West saloonkeeper ducking
behind the bar. It got quiet. There were stares, whispers,
and snickers.

As we made our way to the bar looking for no trouble
at all, one of the locals stepped into the path of one of our
guys and sneered, "I like your haircut." It was the Shelter
Island equivalent of Ned Beatty being told he had "a purty
mouth." To this day I can't tell you what happened next
because I was up at the bar with my back to the action. All

I know is that I felt a shove to the back, and when I turned around all hell had broken loose in the Dory.

It was a scene I'd thought took place only in the movies: Barstools were cracked over backs, pool cues sailed through the air, people were thrown against the jukebox. Apparently these things happen in real life. I'd been in a handful of fights in my life, but this was a *brawl.* It was total chaos. One of my friends was bitten so hard on the leg that the biter's teeth went through his pants (a fine linen slack, I assume) and pierced his skin. Blood pooled in his shoe. I ran into him not long ago on the streets of New York and he assured me that he still has the battle scar.

Local police responded quickly and order was restored without any charges pressed on either side.

We returned home, patched up our wounds, and told stories from the front. Our rallying cry then and forever: "Remember the Dory!"

Geist Date in History

July 4, 1992

On this date, the Geist family once again proudly strutted its love of country, shooting off fireworks from the sidewalk in front of its suburban home. Disturbingly big-ass fireworks for a residential neighborhood. Seriously.

Some call it pyromania. We call it patriotism. Professional skyrockets of municipal magnitude shoot up through a slight opening in the tree branches, exploding in all their gaudy glory, bombs bursting in air. Smoldering ash rains down on the roof of the neighbor's house across the street (they were away) and on the creamy leather seats of a late-model Jaguar convertible. The owner has never attended one of these annual salutes to America and had thought himself fortunate to find a parking space still open right in front of the house.

A crowd of about fifty looks on from the porch, many in disbelief, a few in horror.

There is a police response. The two officers are most pleasant, just saying some neighbors were "concerned" and that it would be best to maybe knock it off. They depart and the order is issued to "commence firing."

The fireworks dealer in New Hampshire, who generally just sold to the trade, had predicted this. He asked, "Whattaya got down there, Bill, twenty acres?" When Bill replied, "About a third of an acre," the dealer suggested, "Better shoot 'em off all at once 'cause the cops *will* come."

The Geist home in Ridgewood, New Jersey

As our homage to veterans of Operation Desert Storm continues, law enforcement arrives again at the scene. They remain calm and courteous, offering that this is the type of thing best left to professionals. "That's it?" Bill replies. "What does it take to get arrested in this town?" They laugh.

By late evening two police cars sit side by side, facing in opposite directions, blocking the street in front of the Geist house. Two lawyers at the party mumble something about being disbarred and leave by the back door. When one of Willie's friends shoots a small bottle rocket at the police cars, the party is officially over. This year.

Chapter 10

Our Birthday Party for Elvis

WILLIE

Before I knew how to read or write, I knew Elvis Presley's birthday. January the eighth. In the photo below,

Jody, Willie, and Libby celebrate the birth of the King

A young Bill shows an early ear for music

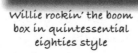

Willie rockin' the boom box in quintessential eighties style

there we are dressed up, wearing sunglasses at night, worshiping at the altar of Cardboard Cutout Elvis to celebrate what would have been the King's fiftieth birthday. January 8, 1985. All your friends were there, Dad, decked out and, as I learned years later, enjoying recreational party favors in a manner that would have made Elvis proud. I was nine. This is what I was up against in life.

The tributes in our family to the King are both grand and routine. You often sprinkle Elvis's "Uh, thank you... thank you very much" into the most mundane of conversations. You throw in the lip snarl and everything.

"Willie, would you pass the butter? Uh, thank you. Thank you very much."

Elvis's *music* plays in our house, sure, but your fascination, I think, is more with the Cult of the King. As one of the great students of what makes America strange (and therefore great), you love the rhinestone jumpsuits, the Jungle Room, the impersonators domestic and foreign, the Elvis and Priscilla salt-and-pepper shakers, the reverential visits to Graceland by pilgrims from around the world, and the frequent sightings of Elvis years after his death, as once chronicled on grocery store magazine racks every week.

I'm hoping that bit of family background makes this next part sound slightly less nuts. When I was in middle school, I owned an audiotape, bought by you, Dad, as a gag at the Elvis Is Alive Museum in Wright City, Missouri (closed for business, 2007. RIP). At least I think it was a gag. The recording proved, as the name of the museum would indicate, that Elvis was very much alive. Elvis spoke hauntingly on the tape about why he had to disappear from public life by faking his own death. The conversation had been recorded surreptitiously in a diner somewhere. Even the biggest skeptic had to be won over when Elvis referred to events that happened *after* his death! How could he know Reagan was president if he weren't... *alive?*

Sometimes I'd lie in the dark at bedtime, with my yellow Sports Walkman on, listening to Elvis explain in crackling audio reminiscent of FDR's fireside chats that he returned to Graceland from time to time and watched from a safe distance as visitors passed through to pay their respects at an empty grave. And oh, how he missed little Lisa Marie.

I should pause briefly and mention that I also listened to music on that Walkman. It wasn't all voices of dead celebrities. Don't want you to get the wrong idea about my childhood.

We don't really go for conspiracies in the Geist family. No truthers, birthers, or "Castro, the Mob, and LBJ!"-ers. We do, though, thoroughly enjoy the more harmless ones. Bigfoot. The moon landing faked on a Burbank sound stage. The death of Elvis. And we're not alone. Whether Elvis is alive has been hotly debated, not just in our living room but on some of the country's most prominent media platforms. Larry King hosted a special hour to settle the matter. Geraldo Rivera did the same, with results similar to those when he cracked Al Capone's vault.

But it was Bill Bixby, of *Incredible Hulk* fame, who performed the most thorough and entertaining examination of Elvis's "death." It was just so earnest. In 1991, fourteen years after the "death" of the King, Bixby hosted the first of two investigative programs entitled *Elvis: Dead or Alive?* If you can't make it to the Smithsonian, I do recommend you watch some of it on YouTube. It's a real-life Christopher

Guest documentary. Eyewitness testimonials. Dramatic reenactments. The president of the Elvis Presley Fan Club as expert witness.

Wherever Elvis may be, his music plays on in our respective homes. Aside from the greatest hits, "Blue Christmas" remains an annual Geist holiday favorite, with Christmas rotation just behind James Brown's "Santa Claus Go Straight to the Ghetto." Dad, you've got a thing for the Godfather of Soul. You've told me about a transformational night in 1969 when you were stationed at Fort Gordon in Augusta, Georgia, the hometown of one James Joseph Brown Jr. I know that seeing James Brown live in a small high school gym in Augusta just before you were shipped off to Vietnam remains one of the highlights of your life, ranking somewhere between the births of your two children. You never do say which one of us James Brown beats on that list.

You taught me to especially love the part of the act where James Brown, "The Hardest Working Man in Show Business," would whip himself into such a frenzy that he would "collapse" onstage. His entourage would rush out, cover him in a velvet cape, and shuffle him off to the wings as the crowd stood hushed. Just then Brown would break free from his handlers, throw off the cape, and rush back to the microphone to continue singing, sweating, and doing 360-degree spins for the people. Now *that* is entertainment.

Another eccentric showman, Michael Jackson, ruled the world during my formative years in the 1980s. Yes, I owned the glittered glove. Don't pretend you didn't, America. I wore it to Glen Elementary School at the height of

"Billie Jean" mania. Lawrence Taylor Giants jersey...blue jeans...Converse...and one sequined glove. There's my third grade uniform. Michael Jackson's music, and that glove that came with it, were welcome in the Geist house. Dad, you were exactly the age I am today when "Thriller" came out. Thinking about the way Christina and I view our own children, I can only imagine the laughs you and Mom had behind my back when the single white sequined glove came out of the top drawer and held my lunch box as I moonwalked out the door to school.

We had a boom box in our basement that served as the stereo. I remember so well listening to our *Thriller* tape over and over while playing basement hockey. I was spooked every time Vincent Price's deep speaking voice came on in the title song:

> *Dahhhhk-ness falls acrosssss the laaaaaand...*
> *The midnight hour is close at haaaaand...*
> *Creatures crawl in search of blood...*
> *To terrorize y'all's neighborhood.*

I got chills just typing that. I'd run up the stairs for a moment when that Price interlude hit, just to make sure Mom was close by when the ghouls started punching up through the tile floor.

Michael's music was a nice addition to an already good stack of records in our house. Zeppelin, the Stones, Hendrix, The Who, Clapton, Wilson Pickett, and James Brown. I remember learning to drop in Brown's improvised screams ("Oww!" "Watch me! I got it!") as I listened to "Super Bad"

or "Get Up (I Feel Like Being a) Sex Machine" while sliding around the floor in my socks, doing a boy's imitation of
the Godfather.

I would sing into a mirror in the downstairs bathroom of
our house on Gateway Road to the new Dire Straits album,
mimicking Knopfler's classic guitar intro on "Money For
Nothing."

We got to move these color teeeee-veeeees!

In that same mirror—and in many mirrors since—I perfected my slithering Mick Jagger dance moves. Those
moves, accompanied by big, pouty lips, made regular
appearances between the hours of midnight and three a.m.
in bars from Nashville to New York City, from 1993 to let's
call it 2007. Mick still has the power to inhabit my body
when the mood (and the open bar) is right.

Over the years I've seen the Stones at Madison Square
Garden and across the river in Brooklyn. I made a strange
road trip with a guy from work to Tampa to see them at
the Ice Palace. That was the first night I ever spent twenty-
five dollars on a T-shirt. I split a bottle of mezcal with my
buddy Murray before seeing the Stones at Vanderbilt's football stadium in Nashville. I rode a double-decker bus with
a group of friends to see the Stones in Atlanta. Then there
were the trips to Atlantic City with Uncle Herb. More on
that later.

Even as the Rolling Stones and co. remained kings
throughout my youth, something was happening in the
culture that caused you and me to part musical ways on
one count. Hip-hop was beginning to leak out of New

York City and into the suburbs. The beats, the samples, the rhymes, the bravado, the clothes, the gold chains, the ghetto-danger-from-a-safe-distance—we ate it up. The first hip-hop record I bought was LL Cool J's *Bigger and Deffer.* The summer after sixth grade, 1987, I knew every lyric to every song. *"The Bristol Hotel: Room 515! The Bristol Hotel: Where that at? Jamaica, Queens!"*

Pretty soon white kids in Ridgewood, New Jersey, and suburbs across the country were straight thuggin' in their own minds, walking around with pants a little lower than they used to be, rhyming like Run-D.M.C., N.W.A., and Big Daddy Kane. Oh, the look on a mother's face when her sweet, WASPy boy sings "Straight Outta Compton" at the dinner table for the first time.

There was a local TV show in New York that we got out in Jersey called *Video Music Box.* It was created by a guy named Ralph McDaniels who wanted to give a platform to hip-hop artists who otherwise didn't have one beyond their neighborhoods in Brooklyn, Queens, or the Bronx. *Video Music Box* became the only show that mattered to my friends and me.

My buddy Eric (previously of soccer taunting fame in this book) and I would race home from George Washington Middle School every day, grab two Dr Peppers and a bag of Krunchers BBQ chips, and settle in to watch an hour's worth of rap videos. In the days before everything was on demand and at your fingertips, you just sat there and hoped Ralph would play one of your favorites, like "Ain't No Half Steppin'" by Big Daddy Kane or "I Got It Made" by Special Ed or "The Symphony" by Marley Marl and the Juice Crew.

When music historians look back to identify the moment

hip-hop exploded from an urban art form to a worldwide phenomenon, they may point to me and Eric, a couple of white suburban kids who sang in the West Side Presbyterian Church choir, sitting on the floor spittin' along as Big Daddy Kane warned us, "Battlin' me is hazardous to health…So put a quarter in ya ass, 'cause you played yourself."

Rap just isn't your cup of tea, Dad. You used to say the term "rap artist" was an oxymoron. I don't blame you for not getting it. It's a generational thing. It would be kind of strange, actually, if my father had been bouncing in his SUV to Snoop Lion or 2 Chainz on the way to the hardware store. I sneak in some when we're together and have made passing attempts to convert you, but mostly we listen to the music we both love.

You're not alone, obviously, in not quite seeing the appeal of rap, but there's no denying that the culture born in a basement rec room at 1520 Sedgwick Avenue in the Bronx is now in the American mainstream. Take a look at the music charts. Look at the slang in our language. Look at the clothes. Visit a bar at any Southern college campus that was segregated half a century ago and watch the place bounce to Lil Wayne. Go to a wedding where the suburban bride and her bridesmaids are going nuts to Biggie's "Juicy," as I did a couple of years ago. Hip-hop has won.

Just as you, Dad, have that strange obsession with all things Elvis, and Grandma E.E. has one with Sinatra, I took my fascination with hip-hop culture a little too far as a young man. Before we were old enough to drive, my best friend Mark and I would have our mothers drive us into an

African-American neighborhood in nearby Paterson, New Jersey, to buy the clothes and accessories we were seeing on TV and hearing about in our music. Mark and I had started to play sports against the two high schools in Paterson: Kennedy and Eastside. We saw in the guys on the other teams the styles and the swagger that we wanted so desperately. So we went to get it. With our moms.

You may remember a moment in the early 1990s when giant baggy polka-dotted pants were popular with rappers. So there was Mark's mom, sweet Sherry, a blonde former beauty queen from Texas, rolling up to these clothing stores in Paterson and waiting as Mark and I picked up polka-dotted pants. We also bought, without irony, four-fingered rings with dollar signs across them. The checkout clerk was utterly confused. Back we went to the bedroom community of Ridgewood, New Jersey, with our baggy polka-dotted pants, our flat-brimmed hats, and, yes, our four-fingered rings. We looked like clowns, and I mean that quite literally. Nevertheless, we put on the uniform, then put on some EPMD.

And while we're on the subject, Tupac and Biggie are totally still alive. You can look it up.

Chapter 11

Willie, Uncle Herb & Mick Jagger: A Journey Down the Garden State Parkway

WILLIE

Before I describe my adventure down the Garden State Parkway with Uncle Herb, you must understand what kind of a Rolling Stones fan he is. As I've said, we Geists love the Stones, but Herb has built a shrine to them in the basement of his home in Stamford, Connecticut. It's a place

Uncle Herb: a rock star on the beach

of worship, really. Glowing only in candlelight and filled with the aroma of burning incense, it's where Herb goes to be with Mick, Keith, Ronnie, and Charlie. Memorabilia covers the walls, loud Stones music plays on a loop, and there is a full bar lit by the glow of a neon sign that reads VOODOO LOUNGE.

I should also mention that in this place of worship, Herb has hung the gold-plated plaque he ripped off the memorial at Jim Morrison's grave at Père Lachaise Cemetery in Paris. Herb viewed it as a collectible for a fan. The French gendarmes viewed it as theft. Herb turned on a burst of speed, darting through the headstones to elude capture. The plaque's final resting place is in Herb's Connecticut basement.

When Herb goes to see the Stones in concert, he dresses as if he's in the band. The thing is, he almost could be. A fit, handsome guy with flowing hair, Herb wears a combination of leather pants, a tight T-shirt, buckled boots, and scarves. It's what Keith Richards would look like if he were still alive (I know, I know).

If Herb sneaked up onstage and started playing guitar on "Gimme Shelter," security wouldn't even question him. He is an honorary Rolling Stone. Years ago Herb and my dad, both with young children then but keeping the dream alive, went to a show at Shea Stadium. They looked good, they felt good, but they did stop to note how difficult it would have been to pick up women with the car seats in the back of the Taurus wagon. Neither age nor children slow Herb down.

Herb, who is my mother's younger brother, is a very successful entrepreneur who has worked in the vitamin and organic herbal supplement business for years. He built up a company and sold it to Procter & Gamble. I tell you this not just to show you that he's a functioning adult who dresses up like Keith Richards from time to time, but also to let you know that he's an expert in the field of, you know, herbal supplements and the like.

So back we go to Atlantic City. It was October 27, 2006. Concert night. Herb got two great seats and invited me to come with him. He even offered to drive. He swung by my office in Secaucus, New Jersey, to pick me up. You hear Herb before you see him most times. As I walked out the front door of our MSNBC building, there he was, blasting his carefully crafted Stones mix on max volume out the windows of his Cadillac SUV. The volume remained at that level throughout the two-hour drive south to Atlantic City. This was not a time for chatting. We had to get in the zone, and we wasted no time doing so.

As I jumped in the car and we squealed out of the parking lot, Herb suggested I pour myself a drink. A drink? I turned around and sure enough there was a fully stocked bar in the backseat. Top-shelf stuff too. Fresh ice. An assortment of Solo cups. I poured myself a bourbon and off we went to see the Stones. At some point along the Turnpike, as we drifted into a rare live version of "Midnight Rambler" or "Tumbling Dice," Herb told me to reach into the panel in the passenger side door. I did.

There I found two ziplock sandwich bags. Written on one of them: "Willie 1." Written on the other: "Willie 2." Inside each was an assortment of pills, some of them familiar-looking, like Aleve. Others foreign.

Checking the clock on the dash, Herb told me to take "Willie 1."

"What is it?" I asked.

"It's a program I put together for this show," he replied.

Oh. A program. Well, he is in the vitamin business, right? Guy does this for a living.

"All of them?" I asked.

"Yeah, all of them," Herb replied, eyes fixed on the road.

My uncle wouldn't steer me wrong, would he? Plus, he's in the vitamin business.

So down the hatch went "Willie 1" in one handful. To this day I still don't know what it all was. Herb swears it was a meticulously measured, and completely safe, assortment of experience enhancers.

I poured another drink, turned the music back up, and felt the wind whip through the car as we powered through New Jersey. As we came around a curve in the Atlantic City Expressway, we could see A.C. in the distance. Granted, it's not like the moment when you see Vegas from the desert after a long drive from LA—"Vegas, baby!"—but when you know the Stones are waiting at the other end, it's better than Vegas. Stones, baby!

As we saw the lights of the hotels and casinos, Herb looked at the clock and said, "Time for the second bag."

Herb's timing and coordination were almost military in their precision. The operation was planned like a shuttle launch. All systems were go for phase two. He'd tailored the sandwich bag for me and determined the precise time its contents should be ingested. A loving uncle takes that kind of time and care with his nephew.

By that time I'd forgotten there was another bag. I was feeling good, but coherent. Cue "Willie 2." I probably looked a bit less closely at this one. It was dark, and the first one hadn't killed me, right? I swallowed it right down.

A two-hour ride, great music, an open-bar car, two sandwich bags full of God knows what, and we were primed and ready for the Greatest Rock 'n' Roll Band in the World. Herb had seats right in the first couple of rows. We'd be able to reach out and touch Keith! This was going to be a night for the ages.

As we pulled up to the venue, revved up, with music on full blast, feeling a bit like Mick and Keith ourselves, there was a surprising lack of activity this close to showtime. Where were all the drunken people in Stones gear? The answer was right in front of us. We looked up at the marquee at Atlantic City's Boardwalk Hall.

ROLLING STONES TONIGHT...POSTPONED

Wait, what? Postponed? That couldn't be right. I'm not sure the Stones fully appreciated that I'd left work early and sped down in a vehicle with a fully stocked bar driven by a guy dressed in tight leather pants and any number of scarves. Oh, also, I had consumed two sandwich bags full of unidentified pills. Come on, guys!

It was right, though. Mick had a sore throat and they'd called the show on doctor's orders. Turned out there'd been some announcements on the radio about the show's being postponed. I looked at my phone and saw a text from a friend at work that said the show was in doubt and I should check into it. But we hadn't been listening to the radio or reading texts from the outside world during our rocket ship ride down the New Jersey Turnpike! We had been getting in the zone…for a show that apparently wasn't happening.

Our spirits low, but being artificially lifted by the sandwich bags, Herb and I parked the car at Trump's place next door to the hall. We couldn't very well turn the car around and leave at that point. We had dinner with a couple of fellow disappointed fans. We spent the rest of the night letting the sandwich bags run their course. We played games of chance in one of America's most depressing casinos. The first signs you're not in the hottest place in town are rows of people sleeping at slot machines, and spots for portable oxygen tanks at the blackjack tables.

So we got no Stones show, we lost a bunch of money at the Death's Door Casino, and we drove home that night in the pouring rain. We even set out in the wrong direction and made it halfway to Philadelphia before realizing our mistake and turning back to start over. Sounds miserable, right? It was a fabulous night. Plus, the whole thing turned out to be a blessing. The Stones rescheduled for three weeks later. So naturally we did it all over again, sandwich bags and all. This time we even got to see the Rolling Stones, but let's be honest, the ride with Uncle Herb was the best part of the night.

That spirit of Uncle Herb, shared by my parents, dictated my early taste in music—good, blues-based, hard-charging rock 'n' roll. I'm lucky to have grown up with that sound filling our house. Otherwise this would have been a long, painful chapter about my childhood with the Carpenters.

Bill…on Herb

With the role models you've had in this family it's a won-der you're not in an orange jumpsuit working at the Joliet prison newspaper writing the Vows column.

And so the torch is passed to a new generation. Who knew that the Rolling Stones of the sixties would still be playing more than fifty years hence and that Uncle Herb, now in his sixties, would still be in the audience?

I finally couldn't keep up anymore. But there you were, Willie, to carry on. Who knew that Herb's enthusiasm would never wane, that he would still fit into those leather pants, that he would go anywhere and pay anything to see the Stones? Wives have been critical of Herb's Stones bud-get overruns, but the weekend wild man is a highly suc-cessful businessman during the week, so…

There ought to be a "Stones with Uncle Herb" service medal with oak leaf clusters (one for each concert). I was there with him in the third row in Atlantic City when the Stones burst onstage and Herb passed out, from excitement and such. I was by his side in Hartford, but my first experi-ence was at the old Shea Stadium in Queens.

It was the first big concert I'd been to in years. I tried to look at least slightly cool, but next to Mr. Leather and Scarves, I looked like his assistant road manager. Everyone shot him a look as he walked by in his silver-tipped boots and studded dog collar bracelet—certain that he must be a rock star. They didn't know he had arrived in the Taurus.

He isn't named Herb for nothing: He's always wearing a fanny pack of healthful, gladdening supplements. Good thing, too, because our booze was confiscated at the gate.

On the way to the stadium we'd stopped at a liquor store where we had to step over a man passed out in the doorway, but with a smile on his face. Well, before we'd heard the famous utterance in *When Harry Met Sally*, Herb said to the clerk, "We'll have what he's having." Unfortunately he'd been drinking Old Crow and Captain Morgan's Spiced rum. We figured the guy in the doorway was onto something, so that's what we bought too. As we were stopped in traffic on the way, a gentleman came up and offered to clean our windshield. Herb, a true humanitarian, gave the man a swig from our Captain Morgan's bottle. I would have preferred that the man had used a straw.

Once there, I felt old, nearly as old as the band, but was heartened to see that most fans arriving at Shea were at least my age, fifty-plus-ers, double-pumping to get out of their Aerostars, wearing relaxed fit jeans and Giants or Jets jackets. As they danced to "Satisfaction" they rather resembled an aerobics class at a Florida retirement community.

One fellow next to me had developed severe back pain from standing so long. Another was high on painkillers left over from his hip replacement. The Stones didn't show for three hours, prompting a woman to yell, "C'mon, we've got a sitter."

Your mom's been to her share of Stones concerts with Herb too, one at the Meadowlands in New Jersey. But who wants to go to a concert in a football stadium? I told Jody to take her binoculars and watch the Jumbotron. Maybe it wouldn't be *so* bad. As it turned out, she and her brother were in the fourth row, center, and your mom gave Ronnie Wood a high five as he passed by. Herb was jealous.

I still prefer kick-ass rock 'n' roll to today's desperately warbling female singers and whispering men. Luckily you like what I like, along with the new stuff.

Rock 'n' roll started a youth rebellion in America. Our parents didn't want us to hear it. "Why can't you listen to Pat Boone?" they'd ask. Bands were nasty and even dangerous. Jody saw the Stones in Chicago in the sixties, when they were outlaws and gave the audience the middle finger. She saw several young women who'd been overcome and were being carried out on stretchers.

Many communities put out the unwelcome mat for Elvis. He was thrown out of Corpus Christi, Texas, where officials said his opening night was "vulgar" and "savage," and that it "promoted juvenile delinquency." When "Elvis the Pelvis" made it to prime-time TV, they blacked out the bottom half of the screen. I remember turning up the volume on the car radio when Little Richard was singing "Tutti Frutti," and my father snapping it off.

So the Herb-Stones baton has been passed to you, Willie, with the hope that someday you in turn will pass it to George and Lucie. The Stones and Uncle Herb will be but in their eighties.

Geist Date in History

August 30, 1992

Just ahead of his senior year in high school, Willie gets his left ear pierced in an act of solidarity with his football teammates. As captain of the team, Willie thinks it best not to tell them that his mother took him to the ladies' hair and nail salon to have the piercing done. Bill had told Willie that body piercing was "something pirates do." Willie was going for a Hells Angels look and ended up with more of a *Charlie's Angels* one. The earring appears in his senior yearbook photo, paired with a pink shirt and a blue blazer, also chosen by his mom.

Willie's high school yearbook photo, 1993. You can see the tough-guy earring his mother took him to get.

~⌒⌐ *Chapter 12* ⌐⌒~

The Talk We *Really* Never Had: Vietnam

WILLIE

*A*mong the many conversations my Dad and I danced around, there is one we never even pretended to have. In 1969, the year after he graduated from college, my dad spent a

Bill, 1968

Jody, Bill, and his long-lost Bronze Star, Christmas 2011

Bill's photograph of a VC fighter surrendering

long year in Vietnam as a combat photographer with the First Infantry Division. It's an important fact of his life he just never brought up, and one I couldn't quite reconcile with the man I knew. My mild-mannered father, a writer, a joker, and a Little League baseball coach, had been on the front lines of war. He'd carried a camera into battle, but also a gun. He'd probably stared down an enemy and used it.

There were things I wanted to know, but I knew my dad didn't want to revisit. His military service made me proud. He'd risked his life for the country, sacrificing in a way I would never have to. I respected my dad for his tour, even if I knew hardly anything about it at all. Occasionally when we've had a couple of drinks on the back deck, I'll get a small piece of his Vietnam story, but he always stops short of opening up.

A couple of Christmases ago, my mother did something incredible. She clawed through the layers of bureaucracy at the United States Department of Defense and finally tracked down my dad's Bronze Star—forty-two years after he returned home from Vietnam. An award lost to the years, opened in a surprise box in front of the whole family. My dad didn't say much as he looked down at his medal, but his face told the story. He doesn't cry much, but he looked damned close that day.

This book gave me an excuse to ask my dad to tell me and you about his time in Vietnam. He writes here more than any of us have ever heard.

BILL

We've never had a talk about my year in Vietnam. I've never had that talk with anyone, even myself. Denial has always worked for me. But here goes.

It was 1969. The worst part of the experience was saying goodbye to your mother. I'd spent most of my high school and college years hoping for a girlfriend but not doing much about it because I feared girls. Heartbreakers, they were. Now I'd found this most attractive woman with a great sense of humor who liked me, and I didn't want to go. Anywhere.

How did I get into this mess? ROTC was compulsory for all male students when I entered college in 1963. It became optional the next year. But my brother, seven years older, had gone through ROTC and was stationed at some *Biergarten* in Germany when he gave me this advice: Everyone's going to Vietnam so stay in ROTC and at least you'll go as an officer.

Consequently, I am about the only person I knew personally who went to Vietnam.

The second worst thing about the Vietnam War was that it was being fought by the army. I hated the army. I hated complete knuckleheads telling me what to do. It was not until I was discharged that I realized knuckleheads telling you what to do was not particular to the military.

I reported to Oakland Army Terminal in California, where soldiers waited, sometimes for days, for their names to be posted for flights to Saigon. As soon as I saw I'd not be flying out that day, I'd hop a bus across the Bay Bridge to Haight-Ashbury, the world capital of hippiedom. I wanted to take it all in: the hair, the head shops, the bizarre clothes, the music clubs—the Matrix was one, where future stars performed—the psychedelic posters all around town for concerts by the Grateful Dead, Jefferson Airplane, Big Brother and the Holding Company (with promising lead singer Janis Joplin), the scent of weed in the air, LSD peddlers on the streets, a flower child dancing naked in the park, all of it. When I talked to people, I never told them my story, they could probably guess by my haircut. They didn't have haircuts.

A couple of days later my time came: to board a bus for Travis Air Force Base for my flight. It was a dark drive through pastoral hills dotted with lights from houses whose owners could afford the view. It's them and us, I thought, the people living in the hills overlooking San Francisco, and the boys on the bus with no more freedom than state prisoners being transferred. But it would be difficult to dash for Canada now.

We flew Tiger Airlines, a private contractor. With stewardesses. I recalled a film they'd shown us of the Viet Cong making bullets by hand, and here we were, not knowing what the hell was going on, flying halfway around the world, being served by stewardesses, to engage a primitive enemy who seemed to be a hell of a long way away to be a threat. We'll go anywhere for a fight.

We landed about twenty-three hours later at an air base outside Saigon, looking out the windows before we landed to see if we could see war. We could not. This was not a war easily observed. Rockets and mortar shells falling from the skies; lethal AK-47 fire erupting from bushes; mines underfoot.

We debarked and were walking solemnly in single file across the tarmac toward the terminal, when I noticed another line of soldiers coming toward us. They were going home, back to "the world" on the "freedom bird," their yearlong countdown to DEROS (return date) down to minutes. Their names would not later appear among the fifty-eight thousand on the Wall in Washington, D.C. By chance.

As the lines passed each other, the vets glanced at us in our starched fatigues and spit-shined boots, with signs of trepidation on our faces, then looked back at the ground. And we looked back at them for signs of something. Their uniforms were faded from the sun, their faces emotionless masks. They appeared weary and not in this moment. And, to me, they looked older.

You'd have thought they'd be jubilant. Or maybe they'd scoff at us as greenhorns. Perhaps give us a thumbs-up, a word of encouragement, pity, or wisdom. Nothing. We in turn said nothing to them: no "Thanks" or "Congratulations." Platitudes. And so the two lines passed silently, without a word. There was nothing to say.

I awoke in a tent the next morning in the vast logistics and human dispersal center of Long Binh. When I stepped outside I saw it. War. Clouds of black smoke. Perhaps there'd been a battle or one of our fighter-bombers had been shot down. I grabbed my camera and, arriving at the scene, asked another soldier what was happening. "We're burning the shit," he explained. This was not colorful military jargon. Vietnam was served by outhouses with fifty-five-gallon drums cut in half and placed beneath them. When the drums were full, soldiers poured gasoline on them and burned the shit. Never saw that in the recruiting brochures.

I had volunteered to go to Vietnam two months early for the guarantee I'd be a photographer. But when I arrived at the duty assignment desk I was told I'd be in charge of a radio communications center in the Delta.

"What about the photography?" I asked.

"Great hobby," the assignment chief replied.

I flew aboard a C-130 cargo plane to Long Xuyên, south of Saigon in the Mekong Delta. I was dropped off alone at a remote unmanned airstrip, where I waited for my ride. It was hot. When I went to pick up my small duffel bag, it didn't budge and the plastic handles stretched out about a foot, like taffy.

There didn't appear to be much war going on there. My job was unimaginably boring, checking the checkers who checked radio dials to ensure all lines of communication were fully operational. But at five o'clock the workday was over. A few of the guys were going regularly to the porch of an attractive and sophisticated sixtyish Frenchwoman, who had managed to stay put or been forgotten when the French were driven out in 1954. She served salty dogs—vodka and grapefruit juice. The guys said they'd take me there the next week. I signed up to teach English at a local school. Life was becoming almost bearable.

One morning the CO called me into his office to deliver the great news. "Well, your wish has come true," he said. "Apparently you wanted to be a combat photographer and now you'll get your chance, with the First Infantry Division.

"I wish to God I was going with you," he said, meaning he wasn't going to be collecting a lot of combat medals or promotions sitting down in the Mekong Delta watching radios.

So it was back to the airstrip and back to Long Binh for a

bumpy one-hour ride to Lai Khê, about forty miles north of Saigon in what was called the Iron Triangle. We pulled up to headquarters, where there was a greeting sign that read: THE FIRST INFANTRY DIVISION. NO MISSION TOO DIFFICULT, NO SACRIFICE TOO GREAT. WELCOME TO ROCKET CITY. This was not a good sign.

It was a substantial base of—wild guess—about a couple of thousand soldiers, set in a former Michelin rubber plantation. I lived and slept in an army-green canvas four-man tent with a wooden floor. There were rocket attacks most every night. After a week or so I was able to not only detect their distinct whistles in my sleep but also get under the bed for a modicum of protection before waking up. When the whistles were very loud it meant the rockets were very near. On one such night, I awoke to find some of that rough wood flooring beneath my fingernails.

On bad nights guys would sleep in the bunker, which was below ground level and topped with sandbags. Particularly guys who were "two-digit midgets," meaning they had ninety-nine days or fewer to go and had begun to consider life after Vietnam. (One day I saw a snake crawl out of our bunker and I never went back in, proving I would rather die than cohabit with a snake.)

In addition to being a photographer I also handled the distribution of photos taken by all division photographers to outlets ranging from the *Stars and Stripes* military newspaper to the Associated Press. Censorship was not too bad, although the powers that be frowned on shots of "Zippo" flamethrowers.

The photo lab had one of the rare air conditioners to be

found anywhere, so it was a popular spot for evening happy hours that consisted of sitting on the floor in a room illuminated by only a red darkroom light, smoking weed, and listening to Led Zeppelin.

As a photographer my job was to determine the most dangerous spot that day and go there. But in Vietnam no one ever knew where that would be. Everybody wanted "action shots" and those were tough to get, what with war being "long periods of boredom punctuated by moments of terror," as they say. I didn't see a lot of action, despite seeking it out. Often when things got rough I'd appeal for a ride home with a high-ranking officer who was choppering the hell out before nightfall. I'd say, "It's urgent that I get this film back."

That didn't always work and I spent several nights scared to death. Nights at small fire support bases were particularly frightening because they were small and there seemed to be the distinct possibility that they could be quickly overrun. Some were. Were there no enemy soldiers lurking out there in the darkness, or a regiment? We shot a lot of flares to find out. You prayed as the flares illuminated the area that you would see nothing.

A bad night would be, for example, one I spent in Quan Loi, up near the Cambodian border. The enemy conducted an all-out assault and several of the attackers broke through our perimeter and went on a rampage. I awoke, realized something bad was going on, and grabbed my .45 pistol. I didn't carry an M16. I sat on the cot in total darkness and aimed the gun at the door of the tent. A man carrying a rifle, and not one of us, was approaching furtively about fifteen yards away. I would kill him when he got to the tent door. But he didn't make it that far before he was shot in the back. When it was over they found among the enemy dead the former barber at the base, who had been seen pacing off distances, apparently for mortar purposes.

Your mom sent boxes of chocolate chip cookies. After he'd seen the first box, Butch, a good photographer who chose to enter the armed forces when a Chicago judge told him it was that or go to jail, brought the next box to my desk and opened it with a machete. A dozen soldiers dove in.

I spoke, if you can call it that, to your mother only once. There were no phones. We signed up to make two-minute calls over a network of amateur radio operators around the world. Our conversation went something like this:

"Jody?"

"Bill?"

"Can you hear me?"

"There's a lot of crackle. I love you."

"What?"

"I love you."

"You're breaking up."

"I love you."

"Me too."

"Bye."

On September 6, I accompanied an armored infantry unit providing security for a supply convoy heading north on Route 13. The stretch was nicknamed "Thunder Road" because of the booming howitzers at fire support bases alongside it. As the convoy rolled north, soldiers sat shirtless atop the armored personnel carriers. They were designed for soldiers to sit safely inside, but most days that was like sitting in a steel pizza oven.

Suddenly someone shouted, "VC!" and several of these tracked vehicles made sharp ninety-degree left pivots and their .50-caliber machine guns began pumping continuous fire into a two-hundred-yard-wide, slightly undulating field of three-foot grasses. Soldiers jumped down off the APCs and began firing their M16s—setting them on "rock 'n' roll," fully automatic. The long, hot battle continued at least forty-five minutes. At one point a soldier took a case of Coke cans off a flatbed truck of soft drinks that was part of the convoy and delivered them to his buddies. I didn't even think of taking any photographs for a while. A soldier had tossed me an M16 and I began firing at the bushes too. The bushes were firing back. I heard bullets plinking off the APC.

When the furious, deafening racket died down, I grabbed my camera and had begun taking pictures when right in front of me, no more than thirty yards away, an enemy soldier in black pajamas stood up with his hands in the air. I instinctively shouted, "Don't shoot!" And they didn't, although they did give me a "Who the hell is this guy?" look. I don't know if I shouted out because I'd been trained that capturing an enemy combatant is preferable to shooting him because of intelligence he might divulge. Or it could have been because I couldn't stand seeing an unarmed young man being shot to pieces at point-blank range. Or it could have even been because I wanted a good action shot.

I got one: the VC with his hands up, a GI in the fore-
ground pointing a rifle in his direction. The photo ran
on front pages in newspapers across the US with captions
like "Hands Up and Don't Make Any Funny Moves." The
"detainee" was a slight young man, no more than a teenager,
who did provide information about troop positions, numbers, and conditions. And he said something that even the
translator couldn't quite get: something like their having
been told that our tanks and APCs were made of cardboard.

Our fighter jets swooped and bombed a tree line just
behind the field where they thought retreating VC might
be hiding. I sat atop an APC as it drove slowly and method-
ically through the killing field. Bodies had fallen in various
positions on the tall grass, many looking artfully posed like
dead soldiers in the movies. Fifty-five bodies.

I looked at each as we inched past. They were all young,
like most of our soldiers. The two groups born on opposite sides of the earth and taught different dogmas, which
they may have believed in or not or probably hadn't really
thought about. They'd never met. They held no malice
toward each other. Yet here they were, as ordered, on this
insignificant plot, here to end each other's lives. I took no
photographs, on this or any other day, of dead young men
on either side.

I hitched a ride back to Lai Khê on a helicopter that was
dropping thousands of flyers saturated with smelly *nuoc
mam* fish sauce to lure VC and North Vietnamese troops
said to be starving. The flyers had a message for them:
If they surrendered they would each receive a motorbike,
absolutely free.

I don't know if I killed anyone in Vietnam or not. I shot at lethal bullet-spewing bushes trying to kill us, and enemy KIAs were later found behind them. But in those cases lots of soldiers were firing at the same bushes. It's called diffusion of responsibility. When I see TV commercials using patriotism to sell military service to impressionable young men and women, it seems there really ought to be the voice of that announcer in pill commercials warning, "May cause neuroses, psychoses, severe burns, paralysis, loss of limbs, premature death, and lifetimes of sorrow." When they announced the fall of Saigon, I went into another room and cried, for the fifty-eight thousand who had died for nothing, not even to serve as a cautionary lesson to never make the same mistake again. We already have.

Geist Date in History

April 15, 2011

Bill Geist gets a star on the Hollywood Walk of Fame. Right next to Paul Anka. And Jane Russell. Tinseltown legend Lassie shows up at the ceremony to honor Bill. This very well may be *the* Geist Date in History.

Bill gets his star on the Hollywood Walk of Fame

Chapter 13

The Family Business: From the *Fisher Reporter* to 30 Rock

BILL

I'm frequently asked if I groomed you, Willie, to become the TV star you are today. Or if we recognized early that you would become one. Nope. Not for the first three decades or so. And even then I wasn't doing any grooming: no hair, no nails, none of that.

Willie, George, and Lucie on the set of *Today*, 2012

Willie's *Tonight Show* debut, 2013

Bill with Jay Leno at the Tonight Show, 1992

Willie interviews Mitt Romney on the Iowa set of Morning Joe during the 2012 presidential campaign as Tom Brokaw looks on

Willie with the Today family

Until you were twelve I'd been a newspaper reporter, even though my father told me to stay away from the business. During the Depression my parents had owned a country newspaper, the *Fisher Reporter* in Illinois. Their memories of journalism were mainly of his lying beneath an old printing press with a wrench and her trading ad space for groceries.

You were always a good writer, Willie. I first discovered this in your letters from camp that so subtly and amusingly described its shortcomings. But I guided you away from newspapers. Not because they were becoming extinct yet, but because I'd had some bad experiences, like being trapped for eight years in the basement office out by the airport of the suburban section of the *Chicago Tribune* local paper, writing about sewer bond referenda. Even when I wrote a popular column on life in the suburbs, I couldn't move up. The legendary Mike Royko liked my column so much that he put his hands around my neck at a holiday party, saying, "You young punks are trying to steal my job!" I was most flattered.

But for a lucky break, a *New York Times* editor reading my humor columns while he was in a vacation mood on a beach, I'd probably be scooping the competition on plans for a new left-turn lane in Bolingbrook, Illinois, right now. I feared you might not get that lucky break.

After I went into TV, I still encouraged you to keep your options open. I remember that when a plumber was working at our house (charging more per hour than Dr. Michael DeBakey was charging per hour for heart transplants), I took you out on the porch and pointed to the plumber's Mercedes sedan. "See, Son, there are other ways to go." I also suggested that instead of having a job you enjoyed and making that your life, you might consider Wall Street, where you'd have a stressful, exhausting job five days a week and spend your boatloads of money on flying in your own plane to exotic foreign beach resorts. You didn't listen. Whew!

What I wanted was what all parents want, I think: for my child to be happy. If that meant I couldn't brag at the country club about my son working his way up to assistant manager of a Shell station, tough.

As for TV, well, you grew up on a set. Our home. We probably shot at least twenty pieces for CBS at our house in every room, basement to attic. Not to mention the garage, where I would do year-end wrap-ups, opening our garage door to reveal significant artifacts and people who'd played roles in the events of the year. The year *Lord of the Dance* was huge, we had a troupe of Irish dancers who'd come from a performance at the Vatican to my filthy garage. Another year it was a group of kids doing the Macarena.

But my favorite was the year 2000, when we included your very witty grandmother, whose name you had forever changed when you were a toddler from Edi to E.E. She was always a great sport and appreciated the absurd. We needed a person of a certain age to sit in the garage throughout the day of shooting, holding computer cards up to the light, looking for hanging chads. It was the least I could do after all those fan letters she wrote to CBS about how fabulous I was, never mentioning (and neither did I) that my biggest fan was my mother-in-law.

Oh, I should mention that lying in a hammock next to her in the garage was Richard Hatch, the famous winner of the first *Survivor* season. Nude. With a magazine covering his not-so-privates. (He got naked a lot during the taping of *Survivor.*) As we closed the garage door in preparation for our opening shot, we asked Grandma E.E. if she was OK with everything and she said, "I raised two sons; I've seen it all."

My first job out of college, Willie, was a six-month stint in the advertising department at Libby's foods on Michigan Avenue in Chicago, where I was assistant to a honcho who was wined and dined by ad agencies. I can vouch for the verity of *Mad Men.* There were indeed three-martini lunches, after which my boss would close his office door and hit the couch, leaving me out in a sea of coworkers with my head on my desk.

I also answered mail: "Dear Mrs. Johnson, We at Libby's foods sincerely regret your finding a thumb in our canned peas. Please accept the two enclosed fifty-cents-off coupons for your next purchases. We hope that you will continue to enjoy Libby's fine line of fresh and frozen vegetables."

The working conditions at my next stop, the army, were atrocious. The Occupational Safety and Health Administration hadn't been created quite yet, and the army had me working in a division where the competition actually shot live ammunition at us. You really need to ask about working conditions during the interview process, Willie.

When I was hired by the editor of the *Chicago Today* tabloid, we moved to Chicago and found an apartment and I went to work, only to find that the editor who hired me had moved to the *Tribune*. The new *Today* editor told me on my second day that he personally wouldn't have hired a reporter right out of school, and put me on the rewrite desk, where I was doomed to fail. "Rewrite men" were the backbone of the afternoon tabloid, with the ability to take a call from Freddie at city hall saying, "The mayor just told Vito to screw himself," then write a full-blown article about it. I could not. There was no place for humor pieces in a "MOTHER OF 14 KILLS FATHER OF 9" tabloid. The executive editor gave me a tip on my way out that there was an opening at the Chicago Transit Authority writing press releases. (That executive editor later taught at Northwestern, where he told a journalism class that letting me go was one of the biggest mistakes of his career. I did not learn of this until twenty years after he axed me.)

I caught on with the *Tribune*, which sounds good, but it was not at that grand, ornate temple of journalism on the Chicago River but rather at the smaller, two-story box-style office in suburban Hinsdale next to a Shell station. The paper was called the *Suburban Trib* and was inserted in the real *Tribune* along with the Kmart ad supplements and other jetsam to be discarded by commuters before they boarded their trains.

After years of my begging for a column on the quirks of suburban life, a new publisher, Bill Rowe, came to the *Trib* and gave me a chance to write about plastic pink lawn flamingos, which seemed to have become extinct but had actually just migrated to backyards; about discovering the yet-to-be-recognized inventor of Twinkies; about finishing third in the Illinois State Fair Bake-Off with my apricot sour cream coffee cake (which would have placed first but for my "uneven nut distribution"); about hookers who serviced an army base that was being closed and spoke out on the weakening of our national defense capability.

On the verge of quitting newspapers, I was hired by the *New York Times* and rose to be writer of the then venerable About New York column, where I wrote about such things as a car with the keys in it that for some reason went un-stolen—in New York City!; about city golf courses with hazards such as abandoned cars and bodies on the fairways; about Donald Trump; about a Korean immigrant who opened a deli on Park Avenue—something one simply does not do—and the full force of the city's government and social elite trying to drive him out.

I moved to TV after Charles Kuralt called me from a pay phone in Texas and said, "C'mon, it'll be fun." If he'd tried to woo me with specifics of the company's great dental plan, I never would have made the move. But I'm a sucker for fun.

In twenty-six years I've traveled the country doing pieces pretty much of my own choosing: on a ninety-two-year-old newspaper publisher in northeastern California who delivers his paper to remote subscribers by dropping them from his old airplane; on a Minnesota town so small it held a "standstill" parade, complete with horses and fire trucks and bands, but instead of the parade moving, viewers walked around it; on two Colorado entrepreneurs who sucked troublesome prairie dogs out of the ground with a sewer vacuum and sold them as pets to Japan.

I think you may be a sucker for fun too, Willie. You seemed to take it to heart when I mentioned that when you have a job like mine you go to suburban parties with businessmen and their wives and you're the most interesting guy in the room. Now that would be you.

ᴄᴏ

A portion of an e-mail written by Bill to Willie at a time when Willie was frustrated by a boss who didn't "get" him or his on-air contribution to a show:

From: Geist, Bill
Sent: Friday, August 4, 2006 9:32 A.M.
To: Geist, William (NBC Universal, MSNBC)

Nobody strenuously objects to beige. When you do things in your own distinctive, colorful way there will be fans and there will be detractors, those who don't

get it, some of them powerful, who don't want to risk
being creative or don't recognize it when they see it.
Your challenge is to charm them into thinking what's
good for you is good for them and, of course, to move
on when those efforts fail.

Love, your biggest fan, Dad

Willie in the Footsteps...

On March 28, 2013, I experienced one of the great thrills
of my career when I appeared for the first time on *The
Tonight Show with Jay Leno*. It was exciting enough just to
walk out onto that stage and talk to Jay for a few minutes,
but there was something more. On June 1, 1992—twenty-
one years earlier—I had sat in the basement of our house
in Ridgewood as a seventeen-year-old high school kid and
watched on television as you, Dad, made the same walk to
talk to Jay. The other guests on your episode were Isabella
Rossellini and Jean-Claude Van Damme. Mine was Kim
Kardashian. Not to brag.

In my dressing room before the show that night, Jay
stopped by as he always does to say hello. He joked about
how old it made him feel to have me there, seeing as you
had been there two decades before, a week after Jay had
taken the reins from Johnny Carson. He brought it up
again on the air. It was a strange, wonderful moment for
me. How could the teenager watching his dad from a white
leather sectional couch in his New Jersey basement be the

same person now sitting in the chair on *The Tonight Show* yucking it up with Jay? How did this happen? *When* did this happen? It seemed impossible. We had come full circle, you and I.

The question I'm asked most, after "What time do you wake up?" is "Did you always know you wanted to be on television, because of your dad?" The honest answer to that question is "No, not really." I knew you had a fun job, traveling the country telling out-of-the-way stories in far-flung corners of America for *CBS Sunday Morning.* You met interesting people, you wrote, performed, and created, and people always wanted to talk to you about what you did. You found American characters the rest of the media wasn't even looking for in places whose populations could generally be expressed in three digits or fewer.

That aforementioned ninety-two-year-old man who delivered the mail in a remote part of California by prop plane comes to mind. So does the one and only resident of Monowi, Nebraska, who served, by default, as the town's mayor, police chief, librarian, and, well, everything else. (She held state-mandated budget hearings with herself.) I personally loved the piece where you shined a light on the vastly under-covered sport of figure 8 school bus racing in Bithlo, Florida. It's precisely what it sounds like. School buses crisscrossing through the infield of a racetrack, slamming into each other. So perverse, and so good.

I know you hate it when you are praised publicly, but one of your great skills is to get America to smile about the people you meet in your stories, without ever mocking them. Those are your people. I feel confident saying you'd rather spend a night at the Iowa State Fair than at a dinner party on the Upper East Side of Manhattan.

It hasn't been all small towns and state fairs, though. You went to Seoul, South Korea; Albertville, France; Lillehammer, Norway; and Nagano, Japan, to cover the Olympics in your own way. You also did some work for CBS Sports' coverage of the World Series. In 1992, when the Toronto Blue Jays played the Atlanta Braves, you started an international incident by implying rather heavily that Canadians didn't understand baseball (e.g., you jokingly showed two Canadian kids playing catch with a hockey puck in a piece that aired during the Series). CBS had to issue an on-air apology to the nation of Canada. How many people can claim they nearly started a war with a friendly nation? It was fantastic.

You arguably did the best work of your television career, Dad, in the days after the attacks of September 11, 2001, when you told the stories of the many victims from our town. You paid beautiful tribute to men and women who lived next door or down the street and never came back to our Ridgewood, New Jersey, train station that day.

As you pointed out, I didn't have to go far growing up to learn how television was made. I'd often come downstairs in our home to find the kitchen or the living room lit professionally, with cameramen, audio guys, and producers scurrying around to set up a shot. Our house, our town, and our family were backdrops for many of those *Sunday Morning* pieces. Whether or not I realized it at the time, TV probably was seeping into my blood. In keeping with the theme of this book, Dad, you never really sat me down and said, "Go into journalism, Son. It's a noble calling." But as I watched you work, journalism had a pretty good head start on the other professions. Plus, we had ruled out tax lawyer and brain surgeon early on for academic reasons.

The thing to know about my dad and his career is that he's not a TV guy. Yes, he's been doing television for nearly thirty years and that's how most people know him now, but he's really a newspaper writer who fell into TV. After years at the *Chicago Tribune* and the *New York Times*, he was wooed over to CBS by the great Don Hewitt, creator of *60 Minutes*, with a big assist from Charles Kuralt. That means my dad didn't come up in life with a hair and makeup team, an army of assistants (or a single one, actually), and the need to be seen and loved around the clock. Come to think of it, he still doesn't have any of those things. You can't find so much as a hint of arrogance in my father. He doesn't big-time people, not because he's worried about his image but because he genuinely doesn't believe he's bigger. Part of that is being Midwestern, but most of it is being an honest-to-goodness humble man. Beyond his huge and obvious talent as a writer and storyteller, my dad's absolute lack of vanity and his respect for every makeup artist, sound man, and hotel clerk he comes across is what I've taken away from him professionally. That doesn't mean I'm getting rid of my eight-man entourage, but I do respect your restraint, Dad.

Kids by nature never really appreciate their parents in the moment. When you're worried about things like who's driving you to basketball practice or what's for dinner, you never fully stop to appreciate what your dad is doing when he's outside that front door. My father had a cultish follow-ing as a columnist at the suburban *Chicago Tribune,* and then a much bigger one at the *New York Times.* I knew that. What I didn't know was the impact my dad had on a generation of young writers. At least once a month, a guest on *Morning Joe*—be it David Sanger of the *Times* or Pultizer winner Ron Suskind, Michael Hainey of *GQ,* or a current columnist for the *Chicago Tribune*—pulls me aside during a commercial break to tell me how he or she studied every word Bill Geist wrote in the paper. One writer told me he would sit at his computer and retype every word of my dad's column to see what it felt like to write that well. It was his way of learning. Another prominent writer sent my dad a long letter telling him how Bill Geist gave him permission to write about his own world by showing him that his seemingly mundane suburban life actually was full of humor, oddity, and fascinating characters. What a cool thing for a guy to hear about his father.

My mom, my sister Libby, and I do our part to keep him grounded, though. We used to recite at the dinner table critical praise he'd received for his books:

"Look! 'America's most beloved humorist' is sitting down to dinner!"

"Good one, Dad! The *New York Times* was right: You really do 'have a gift for uncovering the quirky detail that makes the mundane humorous.'"

"Dad, that was just plain 'Geistian.'"

We joke, but I guess it's time to confess we know it's all true.

Pizza, Lawn Care & Booze

I dabbled in several other lines of work before committing myself fully to journalism. In the summer of 1994, I was the deliveryman for one of Ridgewood's finest pizza establishments. We'll call it Pacino's, to protect both the innocent and the guilty. Pacino's was run by a family that came along ahead of its time, just missing the era in which every hilarious New Jersey family was given a reality show. The patriarch, let's call him Bob, was an older Italian man who ran the joint. He was very hands-on, always upstairs in the kitchen making the pizzas while running the books and the inventory. Good guy, that Bob.

Important detail here: Bob had Tourette's syndrome. His condition didn't manifest itself in strings of expletives. It was more a series of physical tics. The most alarming of these for customers standing at the counter waiting for their orders was one whereby, while making the pizzas, Bob would pause, do a little jump in place, and then slap the big stack of pizza boxes above and in front of him. WHAM! He'd smack 'em good and hard. Scared the crap out of people who were too afraid to ask what in the hell was going on.

Now, anyone who's ever worked in a restaurant kitchen in the summertime knows how hot and crowded it gets back there. You need somewhere to cool down. At Pacino's, that place was the walk-in refrigerator, or "the walk-in box" as we called it. And let's be honest, it's too hot in August even to smoke your cigarettes outside. So here's your visual down in the basement at Pacino's: six people in the walk-in box, most of them related, sitting on boxes of pizza dough arguing about family matters while smoking cigarettes and blowing the exhaust right over the open bowls of sausage and grated mozzarella. It was nice and cool in that walk-in box, but the air got a little thick after a while. Now you know the secret ingredient in our award-winning pizza: Marlboro 100 smoke.

I had two jobs that summer of 1994. I was a pizza delivery guy by night, and a landscaper by day. An enterprising friend from high school had just started his own landscaping company that year, and he hired some of us to be his crew. I had mowed our family's lawn with the little Toro, of course, but I'd never practiced actual landscaping. Now I was responsible for *other people's* yards. I was pushing around big thirty-two-inch Scag mowers capable of shredding a lawn in the wrong hands. Hands like mine.

There were rookie mistakes, certainly—weed-whacking a customer's carefully cultivated flower beds is considered bad form, for example. The idea, it turns out, is to whack the bad stuff—i.e., weeds—and to leave behind the good stuff—i.e., flowers. Another pro tip: The backpack blower is not just used to move your mess to the next-door neighbor's yard. That said, I remain a big believer in blowing your shit into the street and letting cars sweep it away. Who has the time to bag everything you clip?

I worked for my friend's landscaping company for three different summers and learned to like it, actually. There's something really gratifying about mowing a lawn and watching an overgrown mess become a perfectly manicured canvas of stripes and crosscuts. We on the crew got competitive about who could make a backyard look the most like Yankee Stadium. I even stopped whacking flowers. Still, we weren't perfect.

In the summer of '95, we were a motley crew riding three and four across in the company pickup truck. Our buddy Mike entertained us with dramatic readings from O. J. Simpson's new book, *I Want to Tell You*, as we traveled from lawn to lawn. One time, with the boss away, I left a lawn mower in the front yard of a customer's house while Mike and I played one-on-one basketball in the backyard. Long story short, the mower disappeared. Somebody swiped it. Who does that?

There really was no good way to present this news to the boss when he arrived back at the house to pick us up and pack up his precious equipment. We sheepishly rolled everything up onto the trailer. He hadn't said anything yet. Maybe he wouldn't notice.

"Where's the small mower?" he asked. He'd noticed.

Mike looked at me. I was taking the bullet.

"Craziest thing, I'll tell ya…" I said awkwardly.

"Where the hell is the small mower?!" the boss asked again.

"We lost it. We lost the small mower," I replied.

"You *lost* the mower? How do you *lose* a lawn mower?" he asked, not unreasonably. "You're kidding, right? Come on, get the mower."

"We looked everywhere. I think someone stole it," I said as Mike began to chuckle behind the boss's back.

"Are you shitting me? I don't even know what to say. This

has to be a first in the history of landscaping. You *lost* a lawn mower? Go find it."

We went through the motions of looking again, but it was no use. The small mower was long gone. The boss shook his head and we slithered into the pickup riding three wide in silence, having just made landscaping history. I was desperate for a reading from the O. J. book to break the tension.

Our landscaping prowess was on display again later that summer, when the boss's older brother Jeff was running the operation for a stretch. This was back in the days when somebody would drive by your house every year and throw a big phone book in your front yard. Remember that? Remember phone books? Well, this one family in Glen Rock, New Jersey, had really let its lawn go. It must have been knee-high. Maybe they'd been out of town.

As I weed-whacked my way around the yard, Jeff was expertly wheeling the big fifty-two-inch Scag through the tall grass. With my back to the mowing, I was jolted by a big grinding sound followed by a long, loud "Fuuuuuuuuuuuuck!!!!" from Jeff. I'll never forget what I saw as I spun around. My entire field of vision—everything in front of and around me—was a ticker tape parade of tiny shredded yellow pieces of paper. I could see nothing else. It was like a whiteout at the top of a mountain, except it was yellow. It looked like New York's Canyon of Heroes as the boys came home from war or the Yankees celebrated a World Series title. Jeff had mowed the yellow pages as it hid in the tall grass. Wow, what a sight it was.

As I stood mesmerized by the display with my fellow crewmen, Jeff pushed his way through the storm of paper, waving it aside and becoming visible to us for the first time. He shouted at us, "Grab some fuckin' rakes and clean this shit up!"

Jeff was not amused when I scooped up one of the first pieces from the ground and said, "Look, Jeff: dry cleaning coupon! Cool if I keep this?"

He let out one more "Fuuuuuuuuuuuuck!!!!!"

When I graduated from Vanderbilt University in May 1997 with a degree in political science and a minor in French, I was dismayed to learn that there's no such thing as a political scientist, much less a French-speaking political scientist. A heads-up on that a couple of years earlier would have been nice. So now what? I decided to take some time to mull it over back home in New Jersey, where I got a nice deal from you and Mom on room and board.

My best landscaping days were behind me, but I did have another card to play. Four years prior, during my senior year in high school, I had attended the prestigious Metropolitan Bartending School in Nyack, New York. That's right, I took time as a seventeen-year-old high school senior, with college pending, to attend bartending school at night. The classes were held in the conference room of a Ramada. Now, I'm not the kind of guy to wave around his credentials, but my buddy Mark and I were co-valedictorians of the class of the week of April 20, 1993. It was a one-week session, but that takes nothing away from what we achieved at that Ramada. We had a couple of points shaved for an incorrect garnish, but our score of ninety-eight put us at the head of the bartending class. I still kick myself for blowing that orange peel curl. Dad, you light up whenever the subject of my valedictory run at bartending school comes up.

After graduating college, I decided to put that Metropolitan Bartending School degree to good use. I suspect you and Mom would have preferred I put the expensive Vanderbilt degree to work, but I needed some quick cash. I took a job at Wine & Spirit World in Ho-Ho-Kus, New Jersey. The job involved some bartending for customers' parties (the owner, Chuck, had to be proud to have someone with valedictorian credentials in his employ), but the main responsibility was driving the delivery truck. I spent the summer cruising around northern New Jersey making liquor drops in the kind of windowless, two-tone brown van favored by kidnappers in the 1980s. I quite liked being the guy who brought people happiness in a bottle.

The Wine & Spirit World gig was to be a summer job before I moved on to begin my promising career in, uh, something or other. I thought writing for a comedy show would be fun. I looked up to Conan O'Brien, a guy who started as a writer and then got a network late-night show at the age of twenty-nine. So I was going to write for Conan. That was that. I took weeks to put together a packet of original jokes and sketches. I placed my collection into a manila envelope, addressed it to 30 Rockefeller Plaza in New York, and dropped it into the mailbox just across the street from the liquor store. I remember pausing to drink in the moment. That packet and that mailbox would become part of my personal folklore one day. Years later, in the inevitable *Esquire* cover story about my take-over of late night, I'd talk wistfully about the moment that changed everything—when I went from liquor delivery boy to late-night wunderkind by dropping an envelope into a mailbox.

They might even put the mailbox in my museum one day. Man, this was gonna be great.

After a good long wait, I finally got an envelope back from NBC! I'd open the job offer and then take the letter straight to be framed. I'd keep it in my office at 30 Rock forever. Here's what the letter, on official *Late Night with Conan O'Brien* letterhead, read:

> *Dear sir:*
> Late Night with Conan O'Brien *does not accept unsolicited writing material. In compliance with NBC legal policy, no member of the* Late Night *staff has read the documents that accompanied your letter, nor was any portion used on* Late Night with Conan O'Brien. *Thank you.*

All righty, then. That certainly was brief and to the point, wasn't it? OK, plan B. Wait, there was no plan B. In my unwarranted twenty-two-year-old confidence, I'd thought the Conan job was a mortal lock. They hadn't even read my stuff. They'd called me "sir." Jesus. Welcome to the real world, my man.

As my summer job bled into fall, it was starting to look dangerously like a career. You and Mom politely suggested it was time to start real life. I thanked my boss Chuck for a great ride, apologized for a bottle of whiskey that may have "fallen off the truck" here and there, and went looking for a career. I maintain to this day it was a mistake to give up the 25 percent friends and family discount. I know you do too, Dad.

My First Real Job

If you go to college in the Southeast, as I did, there's a good chance you'll end up in Atlanta when you graduate. A group of my friends from Vanderbilt had moved there, so I decided to join them. What to do when I got there was another question altogether. I had some buddies in finance, but given that my understanding of the relationship numbers have to each other ended in the fifth grade, banking seemed like a bad choice. I was thinking seriously about entering the family business.

If you had subliminally planted the journalism seed over the years, Dad, my experience during the 1996 presidential campaign confirmed for me that it was the right one. That summer of '96, before my senior year in college, I had interned at the CBS News Political Unit in New York. I worked under the famed producer Susan Zirinsky, after whom Holly Hunter's character in *Broadcast News* is said to have been modeled. I spent time getting coffees and lunches, of course, but Z, as she is known, had me in the thick of the operation as well. A summer of logging tapes of every candidate event and studying the political positions of guys like Steve Forbes, Lamar Alexander, and Phil Gramm was rewarded with a trip to the Republican National Convention in San Diego. CBS didn't want to pay, so you and I were roommates, Dad.

Every anchor, reporter, and columnist I looked up to was there. Political operatives and pundits mixed in restaurants and bars. There was Dan Rather floating through the crowd at the convention center surrounded by producers, like Sinatra passing through the casino floor at the Sahara. There was Bill Kristol talking strategy at the next table at dinner. There was Pat Buchanan holding a rally down the street. I felt as if I were at the center of the universe.

I was totally professional by day, but I remained twenty-one years old by night, as you were reminded, Dad. One evening of that convention week, I met up with an old friend for a drink in San Diego. That drink ended with me stumbling at some ungodly hour through the door of the room we shared, you asking, "Where the hell have you been?"

"Tijuana, Dad. I've been in Tijuana and I don't really want to talk about it."

Mexican border runs aside, that trip to San Diego punctuated a summer that convinced me journalism was something I was thinking about not just because of my dad, but also because I really enjoyed it. I was ready to give it a shot. The question was, where was I going to get that shot? At Vanderbilt I'd been a sportswriter, then a contributing editor for our school newspaper, the *Vanderbilt Hustler* (it's not nearly as kinky as it sounds, trust me). So when I got to Atlanta I applied for jobs at both the *Atlanta Journal-Constitution* newspaper and CNN, just blocks away from each other downtown. CNN called back, the *AJC* did not. This is how careers are decided. TV it was.

My job interview at CNN's new twenty-four-hour sports network included a written "sports quiz." I had found the one employer out in this great big world who *required* me to know all the trivia I'd spent my life memorizing.

This is what we call in the business "a good fit." I didn't grow up counting sheep to fall asleep, instead naming the last twenty-five NCAA basketball champions, their head coaches, and the tournaments' most outstanding players.

Louisville, Denny Crum, Pervis Ellison...Indiana, Bob Knight, Keith Smart...Kansas, Larry Brown, Danny Manning...Michigan, Steve Fisher, Glen Riiiiiiice...zzzzz...

Now my interviewer was asking me to do the same thing in a professional setting, as if it were work. I could *literally* have answered the questions in my sleep. By the way, if it makes you feel better, I alternated my sleep technique between NCAA tournament winners and United States presidents. That John Tyler–James K. Polk–Zachary Taylor stretch always put me right to sleep.

I began my first real job on January 12, 1998, as a production assistant at CNN Sports Illustrated, a new twenty-four-hour sports news network that was to be the latest to challenge the supremacy of the worldwide leader, ESPN. A good shift at CNN/SI was from four p.m. to midnight, a worse one was seven p.m. to three a.m. Somebody had to watch over that extra-inning Mariners/A's game out West, and most of the time it was the new guys like me. We all worked weekends and holidays, and had strange days off—*Anybody up for drinks at one p.m. on a Tuesday?!* We were paid, technically. My first salary was $23,000 a year. Once Uncle Sam takes his bite out of twenty-three grand, you're looking at a lot of peanut butter and crackers. We lived on a rock star's schedule—we were just missing the money, the fame, the groupies, the talent, and the indoor sunglasses.

CNN/SI served as journalism school for most of us. I went from logging the plays in the games to editing the highlights to helping producers organize a show rundown to writing scripts to producing shows to covering stories and events in the field. All this in the space of about four years. When they pulled the plug on CNN/SI, I stayed on at CNN for a couple more years before deciding I needed to get back up to New York for my next move. I worked for a short time there as a producer on a show called *I, Max* hosted by Max Kellerman and produced by my friends. It remains to this day the only nine-to-five job I've ever held. It was almost disorienting to be fighting my way to work with the rest of the world and then getting home for dinner. Every other job I've worked has involved either getting home at four in the morning or waking up at four in the morning.

The show, while a great time to put on every day with a group of hilarious, smart guys, didn't make it for a variety of reasons. So on February 18, 2005, my wife Christina's thirtieth birthday, I officially was unemployed. At that moment there was no telling what my next move would be. I really had no idea where I was headed. Maybe it was time to get away from the uncertainty of television, where shows come and go like skywriting. I used to think about law school. Or what about one of these Internet startups? Little did I know I was about to become a newsman.

As the members of our *I, Max* crew sent out desperate smoke signals to anyone we knew in the business and assessed our respective stations in life, we connected with Rick Kaplan, who at the time was president of MSNBC.

He'd been president of CNN when I worked there and had just hired Tucker Carlson to host a nightly prime-time political show on MSNBC. He was looking for some ideas.

Rick, it turns out, had been one of the few, the proud... the *I, Max* viewers. He was a fan—a bigger fan than our previous employer, obviously. Rick proposed a wild idea: What if the four of us *I, Max* veterans helped him develop this new show for Tucker Carlson? He thought we were smart, energetic TV producers and he wanted a fresh look at cable news from people who hadn't done it before. His proposal was to hire us as freelancers to help with the development of Tucker's show. We took Rick's offer.

At first we weren't even asked to set foot in MSNBC's headquarters across the river in Secaucus, New Jersey. We gathered every day at my friend Bill's Greenwich Village apartment and spent the afternoon flipping between MSNBC and ESPN Classic, so as not to miss any action in the 1996 Outback Bowl (Penn State upended the Tigers of Auburn, 43–14, as you undoubtedly remember). We'd step out for lunch to strategize over pizza and red wine at Mario Batali's Otto, just around the corner. We'd go back to Bill's place to put together a rundown and write scripts for this theoretical show based on the day's news. This was in the middle of the 2005 papal conclave, so there was a lot to do with white smoke over the Vatican, as I recall. We sent our pretend show to Rick at five o'clock each day.

Rick started to like what he saw. He suggested we have dinner with Tucker. It was a blind date, set up by Rick Kaplan. I'm not sure that any of the four of us knew what to expect. Tucker was the young, bow-tied conservative guy from *Crossfire*—that's all we knew. What we learned that night is that Tucker is charming, kind, generous, crazy smart, and goddamn hilarious. We hit it off completely. If it had been an eHarmony date, they would have put us in the testimonial commercials.

A short time later, Rick offered us full-time jobs running Tucker's new show. It was a big, unfamiliar challenge, but Tucker had convinced us it would be a fun adventure. And let's be honest, ESPN wasn't banging down my door. The four of us signed up with MSNBC. On the first day of work, we piled into one car to make the reverse commute from Manhattan through the Lincoln Tunnel and out to MSNBC headquarters, housed in a cavernous former Liz Claiborne outlet in a Secaucus, New Jersey, industrial park. Somewhere deep under the Hudson River, we became news guys. I have to say, I hadn't seen that one coming when they turned the lights out at *I, Max* a few weeks earlier.

You'll notice that to this point there's been no mention of my being on the air as a reporter or anchor. I reported a couple of spots near the end of my run at CNN Sports Illustrated and for a short time sent some rejected tapes around to local markets, but seven and a half years into my career, I was not pursuing a life in front of the camera. People who end up on television generally are obsessed with the idea. I clearly was not.

As we began to put Tucker's show together, we were looking for an endpiece—something to do for the last few minutes every night. Tucker and I had hit it off in the short time we'd known each other and one day he threw out an idea: "Why don't Willie and I just get out there and shoot the shit?" In that moment, on that whim, my on-camera television career began.

As cultish fans of *The Situation with Tucker Carlson* will recall, I spent the show in the control room. Then during the final commercial break I'd throw off my headset and run into the studio to banter with Tucker about whatever struck us that day, in a segment called "The Cutting Room Floor." One night, for example, we invited a chimp named Mikey to the show. He'd become YouTube famous for some reason or another. Well, Mikey got loose early in the segment and spent the next several minutes running high-speed circles around the studio before parking himself up in the lighting fixtures. That was "The Cutting Room Floor." Apparently no one in the executive suites was watching, so I was allowed to stay on the air.

Less than two years after we got Tucker's show off the ground, another twist of fate. Don Imus, while hosting his daily radio show that was simulcast each morning on MSNBC, made an ugly comment about the Rutgers women's basketball team. It cost him his job at the network. I take absolutely no pleasure in the Imus firing—he was always nice to me—but it was an instant that indisputably changed my life forever.

The next day MSNBC had three hours to fill. Then the next day, and the one after. Desperation set in. Essentially everyone who held a company-issued NBC ID pulled duty on that shift as we scrambled to get our feet under us. Eventually the network settled on the team of Joe Scarborough, Mika Brzezinski, and me. Joe, a former Republican congressman from northwest Florida, had been hosting a nightly prime-time show on MSNBC, but decided he was better suited to political analysis early in the morning. And he wanted me to join him.

I confess I had to be pulled kicking and screaming at first. I was happy doing Tucker's show, working with people I liked, and not as happy about jumping into a new endeavor where the only sure thing was that I'd be waking up at four in the morning. I think even you, Dad, wondered what the hell I was up to. There was arm-twisting from producers, executives, and Joe. I'm glad they twisted.

I call that time in my life "The Brick Wall of Adulthood." I officially joined *Morning Joe* that summer, right around the time my daughter, Lucie, was born. My first child. Almost overnight, I went from a guy with no entangling alliances, as George Washington would have called them, to a man who was waking up in the dark for work and caring for a tiny, helpless human being in his downtime. I'd had a hell of a run from the ages of twenty-two to thirty-two—a decade of decadence in which kicking down the door at seven a.m. had not been unusual. But someone was telling me in no uncertain terms in that summer of 2007 that it was time to grow up.

Beyond just being a good, smart time every morning (despite the six a.m. start), *Morning Joe* has been a great place for me to learn the other side of television. The side in front of the camera. Any success I've had as a television host is owed to many people along the way, but especially to Joe, Mika, and *Morning Joe*. Remember, before I became a co-host of that show, I was still a producer and *occasional* on-air MSNBC contributor. Joe took a pretty big leap of faith sticking me in there. Without the platform we built together, it's pretty damned unlikely I would later be sitting across a table from presidents, prime ministers, senators, CEOs, A-list actors and musicians, or, most impressively to me, Tom Brokaw.

I was an intern gawking at Pat Buchanan at the 1996 Republican Convention in San Diego. At the 2008 Convention in St. Paul, Minnesota, I was on a television set discussing the presidential race with him. How exactly did that happen again? I studied Watergate and the Nixon years in high school, and now Pat was telling me during commercial breaks how he "marched into the Oval Office and told 'the Old Man' to BURN THE TAPES!" *Good God, Pat! Are you legally allowed to tell me that?* "Statute of limitations, Willie," Pat would smile and say.

And how was it that I was at Invesco Field in Denver covering Barack Obama's stadium speech during the Democratic National Convention? And how, four years later, did I find myself sitting in a diner in Des Moines, Iowa, interviewing Mitt Romney as his campaign rolled through town? It all happened pretty quickly. And it happened because of *Morning Joe.*

People ask me how I prepare every day for the show and I tell them, only half-kidding, that I have to know about everything happening in the world that day. My job and my preparation are to be ready for whatever comes up on a wide range of topics and to have something at least marginally insightful to say about it all. My mother taught me to drive on our old Jeep CJ-7 with no power steering and told me that if I could drive that, I could drive any car for the rest of my life. Learning to host *Morning Joe* was a little bit like that—there's no show I can't host after this. And, yes, that is a naked pitch to Hollywood to make me the next host of *Card Sharks*. Just give me a shot, guys.

Because six a.m. wasn't quite early enough to be on television, I asked MSNBC president Phil Griffin to give me the five thirty a.m. slot. Then you *really* thought I was nuts, Dad. That's an insane thing to wish for, I know, but it was a piece of real estate all my own. Luckily, the line for the five thirty gig was a short one. Phil told me to have at it. In the early development meetings, someone said, "Jesus, this show is on way too early." We had ourselves a title: *Way Too Early with Willie Geist*. Four years after running out to the set with Tucker for the first time, I had a show.

With a scrappy staff just big enough to play doubles Ping-Pong on a good day, we zipped through everything the treadmill crowd would need to know for the day—politics, foreign affairs, breaking news, business, sports, weather, and pop culture. With a staff that size, I was still producing—I was on the conference call every night building the show, tweaking the rundown in the morning, writing scripts, choosing video and sound bites, looking at graphics, and doing whatever it took to get *Way Too Early* on the air. At first it wasn't clear that anyone would be rewarding us for all that effort by, you know, watching. Brian Williams used to joke, "You're pretty good. We oughta get you a show." As it turned out, though, there was a good-size audience up at that hour—and not just nursing mothers and degenerates rolling in from the bars, although they were the core audience. Apparently there is a good

chunk of America awake at five thirty in the morning looking for news. People would stop me on the street and say,
"You're in my bedroom every morning at five thirty a.m.!"
My reaction to that comment really depended on who was
saying it. There's a fine line between flattering and creepy.
Soon I began to hear that *Way Too Early* was on in the
Senate and House gyms. People were watching—many of
them sober. Sure, the alternative at that hour was Snuggie
infomercials, but still.

During my time on *Morning Joe* and *Way Too Early*, I got
the chance to do some segments and pieces for *Today*. I
filled in once in a while as the show's news anchor, mostly
on the weekends. Then one day in 2010, I got a phone
call asking if I was available to fill in the following week.
"Sure," I said. "Ann taking some time off?" Ann Curry was
the show's news anchor at the time. "No, Matt is," said the
voice on the other end of the line. I must have paused awkwardly because the next thing I heard was, "You're filling
in for Matt." As in host Matt Lauer. I was being asked to
host the *Today* show.

I had the good fortune of co-hosting that first morning
with the wonderful Meredith Vieira. I remember her pat-
ting me on the back and smiling at me as we went to air.
I learned later she was just hitting on me aggressively, in
what would become a pattern of abuse that kept NBC lawyers busy most days.

I don't care how much TV you've done or how cool a
customer you are, the first time the clock hits seven a.m.,
the *Today* theme music you've heard your whole life starts
to play, and you turn to see *the* Meredith Vieira sitting next

to you, it's a moment. Next thing you know you're trading witty banter with Al Roker—you know, the weatherman who formerly existed only inside your TV set at home.

Not a day goes by when I don't wonder how the hell I ended up sitting at a desk with Matt Lauer, Savannah Guthrie, Al Roker, Natalie Morales, Carson Daly, Hoda Kotb, and the one-and-only Kathie Lee Gifford—playing in the same lineup with the New York Yankees of network morning television. When young people interested in television ask me how I got there, I have to laugh.

Write this down, kid: "Be a sports producer for seven years, have your network pulled off the air, move to New York, get your show canceled shortly thereafter, be unemployed for a while, have an executive at a cable news network like your canceled sports show and invite you to produce a news show, then have the show's host suggest you be on the air for a couple of minutes, get Don Imus to spout off on women's basketball, go from producing news to co-hosting a new and ultimately successful cable morning show, talk your way into a predawn show of your own, then have someone at the Today *show call you one day and ask if you can fill in for Matt Lauer." You got all that? All right, now go get 'em!*

There's no following that path. All I know is, seventeen years after dropping that packet for Conan into the mailbox outside the liquor store, I'm walking into 30 Rockefeller Plaza for work every day. Just the way I planned it, Dad.

Geist Date in History
July 15, 1985

In an effort by Willie's mother to balance his growing obsession with sports, he begins his summer stock career. His first role is a groundbreaking one. He plays the only boy in Miss Hannigan's all-girl orphanage in the classic *Annie.* He is, theatrical records show, the only boy in the

Willie hits the summer stock trifecta: short shorts, knee-highs, and jazz shoes

Willie nails his choreography...

...and struts in his Hulkamania T-shirt and Air Jordans

orphanage in any production of *Annie* ever. After shattering that glass ceiling, Willie goes on to "star" in productions of *The Sound of Music* (Friedrich), *Really Rosie*, and *Fanny*, in which he wears tiny short shorts, knee-high socks, and jazz shoes with a slight heel.

Chapter 14

Parkinson's:
The Denial Treatment

BILL

There's never been a good time for me to deliver bad news, especially not to you and your sister. As you know, I'm a private person. I was raised to suppress the

Bill's Parkinson's announcement on CBS Sunday Morning, with Daphne

Bill and Willie with Michael J. Fox

whining and keep things sunny-side up. For the past twenty years, only your mother knew that I have Parkinson's disease. She says the only reason she finally told you and Libby was that you thought when I took long naps every afternoon—Parkinson's drains you—it meant that I didn't want to do what the family was doing, or maybe that I just didn't like being around you two. That was crushing to hear.

When I finally did discuss it with you at a Rose Bowl game a few years back, I told you I didn't want to be the subject of pity. You said no one could pity a man who had just walked five miles to and from the Rose Bowl!

I lived in denial, which had always worked for me. I didn't want to think about Parkinson's, didn't want to let it into my life, into my house, didn't want it to be the first thing people thought of when they saw me. I didn't want my office to know, didn't want to disqualify myself from moving up, although certainly my field producer, Amy, who traveled the country for fifteen years with me and saw me taking pills, knew something was up.

Moreover, I didn't want you and Libby worrying about it: my having it, your inheriting it. Undoubtedly you saw that I was walking funny. And squirming. Holding my hands in awkward positions. People notice, especially when five or six million of them are watching you on TV. They'd see a twitch and send me an e-mail or put it on Twitter, at first as a question: "Does he…?" "Is it possible he…?" Then it becomes the first several items on your Google search (which I haven't checked now in five years). I thought I was hiding it pretty well, but when I looked at video of myself, I knew I wasn't fooling anyone.

Unfortunately, denial doesn't work so well with disease. You try to keep it out of your head, but it keeps reminding you it's there. There are symptoms. They worsen and multiply. You can tamp them down with drugs but they keep popping up.

I withdrew, holing up in my office with the door closed, working more at home and not seeing old friends because I wanted them to remember the old me, not the new whoever-I-had-become me. In public I make a concerted effort to look "normal," but my movements don't flow easily, and at times neither do my thoughts. Sometimes my feet stick to the ground.

Parkinson's is weird. In addition to all the physical ailments, it causes depression and flattens your emotion. The old sparks become wet matches.

The last thing I want to be is a drag. I've always been the one to cheer everyone up. Make them laugh. Fans would write to me: "They were reading your column on the radio and I had to pull off the highway I was laughing so hard"; "People on the bus thought I was nuts I was laughing so much"; "I fell to my knees in front of the TV laughing and pounding the carpet."

∽

It was at a book signing event in Richmond in 1992 that I first noticed my signature getting tighter and smaller and sometimes illegible.

"Sorry," I'd say to the signees, "I'm recovering from a broken wrist."

"That's too bad," they'd say. "How'd you do it?"

My answers were whatever came to mind: "Skiing…

in France" or "Playing football with the kids." My mending broken wrist was the excuse I used for years. In more recent signings I finally went so far as to say, "Sorry, I'm having a little neurological problem with the hand."

I visited a neurologist who said I was experiencing writer's cramp. She did all manner of tests: hand, foot, eyes. There was an MRI, an EEG, an EKG, and a series of tests in the examining room that involved pricking my hands, feet, and thighs. She repeated this with electric shocks. She put me on a couple of drugs. She said I had mild Parkinson's disease. I told the doctor that we were moving to New York and she gave me a referral. Her final words to me: "Good luck."

Six neurologists, twenty years, and about a dozen different medications later, it's still pretty much "Good luck." There is no cure, just trying new combinations of somewhat effective and promising new drugs, one to six times a day. The next approach might be drilling a hole in my head, which always causes me to think of Black & Decker.

The uncertainty haunts you. You don't know what will happen to your body, nor how soon. And how much of this is owing to Parkinson's and how much to what one MD diagnosed as my "rotten" back, and how much to the fact that I'm getting really, really *old*? I'm in denial about that too. Several of my high school friends are six feet under.

I go for appointments with my Parkinson's doctor (as distinguished from my battery of other doctors: skin, back, eye, heart, etc.), and I see patients in the grip of the late stages of the disease. At first I think, "I have nothing to complain about. I shouldn't even be here." Then I think,

"That's me in a few years." I go home and we plan the trip to Africa we've thought about forever.

Deep down, beyond the realm of rationality, I somehow feel that it's all still temporary. I am always a little disappointed and angry when it takes ten minutes to button my shirt. I yell "Fuck you!" at the disease. I hope your kids haven't overheard me.

Willie on Parkinson's

I've told you this before, Dad, but the day you announced to the world on national television that you have Parkinson's disease—Sunday, July 1, 2012—was my proudest as a son. The star on the Hollywood Walk of Fame was pretty badass, and I don't mean to diminish your third-place finish at the Illinois State Fair Bake-Off, but admitting to so many people what you'd denied to yourself for so long was a hell of a brave thing to do. We sat in the living room together that morning—you, me, Mom, and Christina—watching, applauding, and crying a bit. It had been a long time coming.

I agree we were better off not ever having the "birds and bees" talk, but the Parkinson's conversation definitely was one we should have gotten around to sooner. When your early, mild signs began to show, Mom told us you had a "neurological thing" as if it were something that would pass. I look back now and wonder why I didn't ask more questions—of Mom and of you. You were trying to protect us, I guess, hoping the disease somehow would go away and we could get on with our lives as normal. I can't remember the moment Mom told us you had Parkinson's, maybe because it was so unsurprising. We knew by then what our eyes had been telling us.

I do remember the first time I noticed you slowing down. We had a white Jeep Cherokee in the early and mid-nineties with an automatic sunroof. Don't ask me why, but it registered with me one day when you guided your hand slowly up to press the button to open the roof. It was a strange thing for me to store away in my mind, I know. Like a lot of little things that followed—the naps, the occasional reach into a pocket for medication, the subtle social withdrawal—I chalked it up to Dad just getting older and slowing down. Except you were only in your early fifties. I should have known something was up. But I didn't. Hereditary denial, I guess.

Once you told Libby and me the World's Most Obvious Secret, we encouraged you to tell everyone else. That took some time. Then one summer morning in 2012, I woke up to a bunch of e-mails and tweets containing well-wishes from friends and strangers about "your dad's news." What the hell were they talking about? Turns out you'd decided to let the world know you have Parkinson's disease in a late-night Facebook post—a response to an inquiry from a virtual "friend." Social media, insomnia, and, I'm guessing, a little Scotch conspired to get the word out. Whatever it takes.

Whether or not you recalled making the announcement in the wee hours, the outpouring of love and support you got from the people who have watched and read you for

decades vindicated your decision to "come out." Then
there are the millions of PD patients who drew inspiration from the fact that you've worked full-time for years
with the disease—appearing on television, no less. They told
you as much in thousands of letters and e-mails. And still
today, nearly two decades into your fight against Parkinson's, you're working like a thirty-year-old, traveling the
country, telling stories, and making people laugh. Doing
your thing.

In case anyone reading this wonders if you have a sense
of humor about all this, a quick story. The fall after you
made your announcement, you and I were invited to speak
at the gala for the Michael J. Fox Foundation, the phe-
nomenal Parkinson's group. In a hushed Waldorf Astoria
ballroom full of New York's most famous and glamorous
people, you talked about living with a disease that, among
other things, causes tremors. The audience was waiting for
something sentimental and reflective. You began with this:
"I thought at times about ending it all." The room went
silent, the group stunned by what sounded like a dark con-
fession. I knew better. You continued, "But I was afraid
if I tried to shoot myself, I'd miss." The room erupted in
laughter. A little sick, Dad, but funny as hell. Just like you.

Geist Date in History
February 1, 1968

Bill is sitting in KAM'S, a campus bar at the University of Illinois in Champaign, drinking beer, when a gorgeous, tall blonde comes sauntering over with a cigarette between her fingers and asks in a mock-sultry voice, "Got a light?" Bill never would have had the confidence to approach a girl of this grade. Turns out she's a fan of his poetry, which unbeknownst to him is making the rounds. A sample:

Jody and Bill (fairly recently)

THE ARMADILLO
By Bill Geist
The armadillo is an ugly thing.
Unlike the songbird, it does not sing.
It won't do tricks in your yard.
It just lies around...and, is hard.

They made a date to hear LSD proponent Timothy Leary. It went so well that Bill invited her to his fraternity's Fiji Island party, where members dressed in loincloths. Unfortunately, Bill started celebrating very early in the day and by the time the party rolled around Jody (to her eternal credit) had to go without him.

Geist Date in History
September 7, 1986

After a move across town in Ridgewood, New Jersey, Willie is the new guy at George Washington Middle School. In the first few minutes of his first day of school, he spots in Mr. Kaplan's homeroom class Christina Sharkey, recently of Willard Elementary. At eleven years old, he has a pretty good idea she's the One. As it turns out, she is. Sixteen years later, Willie proposes to Christina in that same classroom, with their old principal George Neville presiding. She says, "Yes."

Willie and Christina's junior prom, 1992

Chapter 15

Bend but Don't Break:
The Geist Parenting Style

WILLIE

The Bill Geist parenting style is captured nicely in a scene from the Ridgewood Biddy Basketball Banquet, circa 1985. The Biddy Banquet was an annual gathering at

l and Willie, May 1975

Lucie and George on a
regular visit to the NYPD's
20th Precinct

Willie and Lucie, June 2007

Dad, we have to
go on a call!

Bill and his mother, Marjorie

Little Willie with his
beautiful mother

Towhead Willie on the first
day of nursery school

one of northern New Jersey's wide selection of mob-run event facilities ("Have your next event with us…or else"), where achievement in grade school basketball was recognized with trophies and baked ziti.

This year, in addition to the usual ceremony—the presentation of the Biddy colors, the State of Biddy address from the commissioner, and the awarding of the season's Kid Who Seemed Like He Tried Pretty Hard Most of the Time plaque—there was to be a special guest. Rumors circulated for weeks leading up to the event. Would it be Knicks star Bernard King? Maybe head coach Hubie Brown? We'd even be happy with rebounding machine Ken "The Animal" Bannister. Or perhaps a member of the home state Nets? "Chocolate Thunder" himself, Darryl Dawkins, would have brought down the house. Whichever guy it was, it was going to be great for a roomful of basketball fans. A can't-lose proposition.

So when the announcement came from the podium that it was time to welcome our guest, all eyes went to the main entrance of the ballroom at Unnamed Mob-Run New Jersey Event Facility. The music started, the doors flew open, and in a burst of enthusiasm, out came…a furry dragon in a Nets uniform. Oh Jesus: It was Duncan, the Nets mascot.

During its long run at the Brendan Byrne Arena in East Rutherford, New Jersey, the Nets organization did whatever it could to distract the fans from remembering they were watching a bad team in an empty arena in the middle of a New Jersey swamp. Larry Bird called it the arena he hated most during his long career, saying of the fans, "It's as if they're not even there." That wasn't just your impression, Larry. They *weren't* there. It was the kind of place where you could see a friend across the arena during a game and, I kid you not, yell across the court to make postgame plans. At any given game, a quarter of the crowd was composed of Boy Scout troops and school groups on mandatory field trips.

There's no particular connection, as far as I can tell, between a friendly dragon and the New Jersey Nets. I just don't think anyone ever cared enough to challenge it. Maybe the Nets got a deal on a rejected *Sesame Street* costume. Duncan danced, threw T-shirts to the crowd, and blew fun streamers out of his oversize nostrils. And now, in a big, exciting surprise, he was here to electrify the Biddy Banquet. He did, although not in the manner he had anticipated.

Needless to say, the room expecting the great Bernard King was a little disappointed to see a guy in a furry dragon costume. Remember, you're dealing with elementary and middle school boys, known colloquially as "punks." So when Duncan began to dance and weave his way through the tables, stopping only to perform one of his signature pranks on an unsuspecting Biddy dad, the cold, hard dinner rolls at the center of every table became ammunition. First one table of troublemakers hurled their bread at Duncan, drawing a playful reaction from the mute dragon. The first shots of the revolution had been fired. Every kid within arm's reach of a bread basket unloaded on Duncan. The furry Nets dragon had walked into an ambush—a relentless barrage of carbs. Servers dived for cover. Fathers shielded young children. Innocent victims were caught in the cross fire.

As the scene devolved into something that looked like Altamont in '69, the commissioner took to the microphone to restore order. He insisted the boys stop pelting the evening's special guest. And there was paternal discipline. Fathers grabbed their sons sternly, some of them leading their boys out of the room. I hadn't yet felt a tug of the arm from my dad by the time Duncan passed our table. I had a clean shot. Did I take it? As Jack Nicholson said under questioning in *A Few Good Men,* "You're goddamn right I did!" Code red on Duncan.

I reared back and threw some high heat into Duncan's back. Nothing before or since ever felt so good. I knew there would be consequences. That was part of the rush. I turned and looked at my old man to see if I was in trouble. I was not. I was the opposite of in trouble. While other dads were calling for a cease-fire, Bill Geist was howling with laughter. I got the distinct sense he had to sit on his hands to suppress the instinct to join the attack. My father couldn't—and can't to this day—resist a good, mischievous laugh. Even when a kindly, furry dragon is being brought to his knees by the bad boys of the Biddy Banquet. Thanks for letting me beat up the Nets mascot, Dad.

"I'd say you've had enough!"

Another page from *The Bill Geist Parenting Manual.* Back in the days before a thousand cable TV channels, the Internet, and everything on demand all the time, kids didn't have a lot of choices in entertainment. My kids know every word to *Toy Story, Cars,* and *Monsters, Inc.,* but I can't say I have many young AV memories beyond maybe a Muppets movie and *Sesame Street.* The first movie I remember watching on a loop with you, Dad, was a hell of a long way from Kermit and Big Bird. You brought home a VHS copy of Mel Brooks's *Blazing Saddles* and told me, "*This* is funny." Age-inappropriate for an eight- or nine-year-old? Sure, but good God, were you right.

When I watched the campfire farting scene the first 250 times, I wasn't sure how anything else ever could be funnier. I had been to the comedic mountaintop.

"How 'bout some more beans, Mr. Taggart?" says one of Taggart's men as they sit around the campfire shoveling beans into their mouths and making orchestral music with their rear ends.

"I'd say you've had enough!" replies Taggart as he waves the air with his hat.

I wore out that VHS tape by rewinding the farting scene and playing it over and over. I carried word of this tape back to Glen Elementary and after school gathered friends in our den to watch. I was spreading the gospel. *Blazing Saddles* also gave us Mongo punching out the horse and the ladies of the town's church choir singing a hymn that ended, "There's no avoiding this conclusion/Our town is turning into shiii-iiit, oh."

Blazing Saddles was not a parenting outlier for you, Dad. You took me to see *Beverly Hills Cop* when I was in fourth grade. Fourth grade! In the space of two magical hours, Eddie Murphy taught me the wonders of the f-word, I saw boobs in a strip joint, I watched dozens of people get murdered, and I learned a good bit about the international cocaine trade. You and I went to the movie on the condition that I not tell Mom. She figured it out, though, when I walked around the house dropping f-bombs in Eddie Murphy's voice. Also, when you bought me the *Beverly Hills Cop* VHS tape that Christmas for further review. I honestly don't have much childhood recollection of Big Bird or Cookie Monster. But I can tell you every word Axel Foley ever said.

All those laughs and all that lenient parenting almost make up for the losing Pinewood Derby car you made me in Cub Scouts that year. I'm still working through the pain of the last-place finish.

A Rough Start

My own turn at parenting began rather inauspiciously, truth be told. I was there in the room, of course, on the wonderful June day when my daughter, Lucie, was born. I could see Yankee Stadium out the window of the delivery room that afternoon, where the Bombers were capping a nine-game win streak with a 7–1 dismantling of the Arizona Diamondbacks. A-Rod went three for four with a couple of RBIs. Andy Pettitte got the win. It was Flag Day too. The stars were aligned for our little girl.

It's been said many times, but the birth of a human being is the single most overwhelming moment life has to offer: In the space of seconds, your life shifts outwardly from your body to the little wailing person who has just appeared in the room as if in a David Copperfield magic trick—where the hell did *she* come from? I think my wife, Christina, would tell you I was steady and solid in the delivery room, but less so a couple of mornings later when it was time to leave the hospital.

The night before we were to be handed the keys to our daughter, I went out to celebrate the birth with some friends. I recall bourbon—there is always bourbon—and champagne, and maybe more. The hospital wristband is always good for a couple of free drinks. I had stayed by Christina's bedside holding little Lucie until closing time in the maternity ward on the second night of her life. I was to return early the next morning to scoop up my ladies and get on with the business of parenthood. Well, the drinks often start flowing as you celebrate the dawn of a new life, you lose track of time, and it gets late. Again, all in celebration of Lucie (*he has reminded his wife over the years*). Next thing you know, you open your eyes, the sun is out, and you're two hours late for one of the Kodak moments of your brief time on earth.

I showered quickly to wash away the sins and hauled ass up to Christina's room at Columbia-Presbyterian Hospital in Washington Heights. Her bag was packed, Lucie in her arms. There was no point in apologizing. "Sorry" couldn't cover this one, but, hey, I'd been out celebrating our baby, right?! No? OK. Maybe it was wickedly smart of me to set the bar low on the first day. I've looked like a model parent by comparison ever since.

I'll never forget walking out of that ward with Lucie strapped into her brand-new green car seat for the first time and having a nurse say to us, "Good luck, guys!" Good luck? Good luck?! That leaving-the-hospital-with-a-baby "Good luck" is the heaviest "Good luck" there is. Good luck keeping that little person alive. Good luck teaching her how to be a functioning human being. Good luck not screwing up her life! Couldn't those nurses just come home with us? Forever?

They didn't come home with us and thanks to a wife with maternal instincts and confidence that I will never fully understand, we've done pretty well. Six-year-old Lucie is smart, beautiful, funny, and curious about her growing little world. She reads, she writes, she solves math problems, she draws portraits, she dances around the living room, she tells good stories and bad jokes, she swims, she rides the subway and a two-wheel bike, she orders dinner in New York restaurants with manners, she has outfits, she disciplines her little brother and watches over him, she hugs, she kisses, she holds my hand in public, and she generally walks on air. I just kind of feed and bathe her occasionally.

When Lucie first started to talk, we were a little worried we were raising the world's next tyrant, destined to end up at a war crimes tribunal somewhere. Parenting her was like working for Anna Wintour. Lucie preceded most of her commands with the word *lemme*.

"Lemme take a walk!"

"Lemme have some pasta!"

"Lemme watch the Wiggles!"

"Yes, ma'am," we'd say, as we fed her grapes and fanned her with palm fronds. Luckily her tyranny appears to have been a phase.

Use the Cops

Let's be honest, Dad: Sometimes the job of parenting is too big for any one or two people. Sometimes you have to call for backup. We call it "third-party discipline." Anybody in a uniform will do. Police officers, firemen, bus drivers, airplane pilots, park rangers, lifeguards, dental hygienists, gas station attendants, movie ticket-takers, chefs, pharmacists, and anyone wearing a hard hat are all soldiers in the war against our own children.

You want your kids to know that someone they actually respect and fear is watching at all times (i.e., not you). Christina throws out "The manager is watching!" at least once a day, whether in a restaurant, a bookstore, or a place that doesn't have a manager, per se. *Manager* is an umbrella title of authority that gets George and Lucie's attention. On the same day that I write this, Christina turned and looked at the pickup window at our diner and said, "George! The chef is watching through the window!" George stopped pouring Sweet'n Low down his pants immediately. Now, sometimes the third-party discipline method has to be taken to the extreme.

We live in New York City near the NYPD's Twentieth Precinct. The officers there are very real cops fighting very real crime. It's New York City. In addition to their other responsibilities, we've given them jurisdiction over our son. If there's a problem that really needs correcting, we swing by the precinct with George. That's right, we threaten our four-year-old with a police booking.

Before you call Child Protective Services, you should know it takes a lot for a visit to rise to this level. We take George to the police station much more often under happy circumstances. The officers there humor us and give George an official NYPD patch once in a while. He must have a dozen. When George and Lucie race down the sidewalk on Eighty-Second Street and skip into the precinct to visit their heroes in blue, the generally sullen visitors in the lobby wonder what the hell these two happy little kids are doing in their world of pain. The adults are there to report their cars stolen. My kids want a patch and a free brochure.

Any brochure will do. They're not choosy about their law enforcement literature.

It's always a fun game to see which informational pamphlet they'll come outside with. The most frequent choice is the one about bicycle theft. Second is the domestic battery one...written in Spanish. So if you see a little blonde girl in a cotton dress skipping along the streets of the Upper West Side carrying a Spanish-language Crime Stoppers brochure, that's our Lucie.

But when George has taken a whack at his sister or been tough on Christina, the experience is very different. I lead George into the precinct by the hand as if he's a perp arrested in a preschool sting. There will be no patches or brochures. The guys at the Twentieth know us now and they play right along. We self-report the offense to the towering officer as three-foot-tall George stares up in awe at the uniform, the gun, the badge—the whole NYPD package. The officer shakes his head and looks down at George, who is backpedaling at this point. In a perfect New York accent, we get:

"George. You can't hit your sista. Undastand? Come on, buddy."

"George, you gotta eat those vegetables, big guy. Come on, whatta ya doin'??"

I've read all the books and heard from all the experts, and I defy you to find a more effective method of discipline than putting your child toe-to-toe with the New York Police Department. Buys us a solid week of good behavior. And some of the information in those brochures really is quite helpful.

"You're fired!"

As every parent of young children knows, there are moments each day when you have to suppress a laugh before telling your child he or she is doing something terribly wrong. You've joined me in many of these with your grandkids, Dad. Some of our biggest laughs came when George went through a phase of firing people. If he was angry or frustrated with someone he'd look right at them and shout, "You're fired!" Like Trump in the boardroom.

The terminations usually came as the punctuation to a tantrum—the big finish. George has fired both of his grandmothers—Jo-Jo and Nonna. He's fired his own mother. He's fired his swim coach. That last one went down when he decided about halfway through the lesson that he was finished. As the coach tried to coax him to stay in the pool, he climbed the steps, turned around, and said, "You're fired!" Then, as others around the pool were heard laughing, he fired all the spectators before storming off with his arms crossed. Just like that, five or six adults lost their (unspecified) jobs. He's ruthless. Doesn't even go through HR first.

The problem with his firings, though, is that he generally turns around inside of ninety seconds and asks the person he has just canned for a favor. It's hard to respect a boss who fires you and then quickly says, "Can I have a red Popsicle?" He runs a pretty strange shop. Lots of turnover.

We were free to laugh out loud at George's recent preschool parent-teacher conference. His teachers raved about him for a good long while, but we knew it couldn't all be so rosy. He was three, after all. We waited for the other shoe to drop, but it wasn't so much a shoe as his pants. His teacher Ms. Walsh said, "Well, there is *one* thing."

"Oh no," we thought to ourselves. Is he hitting? Eating crayons? Putting firecrackers in the toilets? Just lay it on us, Ms. Walsh.

"George has been doing a good job going to the potty at the school," she said.

OK, good start. Where's this going?

"It's just that when he comes out of the bathroom, he doesn't pull his pants up. We're seeing a lot of his tush."

Christina and I burst into laughter. The teachers joined in. It's not just that he doesn't pull up his pants after he goes to the bathroom, it's that it doesn't bother him a bit. He comes out to the common sink in the classroom with his jeans around his ankles and washes his hands while the class gets a full view of his little twin hams. Then he dries off the hands and does the pants-around-the-ankles walk to the play area and asks, "Are the blocks available?" (Pronounced "avay-vubble.") Public nudity was the one check in the "Needs Improvement" box. We've spoken to him about it.

"Leotards!"

Once a year or so, Christina goes away on a trip to get the hell away from us. Trust me, she earns that trip. That means I'm home for forty-eight to seventy-two hours with George and Lucie. Not such a big deal, you'd think. They're my kids. It's not as if I haven't ever been alone with them. But

I do need a little refresher on the habits of these strange creatures. As Christina rolled her bag out the door for the most recent of these trips, the following exchange took place:

CHRISTINA: You good?
WILLIE: Yep. Have fun. We'll see you on Sunday night.
CHRISTINA: OK, love you guys.

Just as the door is about to close, Willie yells to Christina.

WILLIE: Wait, babe?!
CHRISTINA: Yeah?
WILLIE (NOT FACETIOUSLY): What do they normally eat?
CHRISTINA: Are you serious?
WILLIE: Kind of, yeah.
CHRISTINA: Goodbye.

That's one you'd really like to have back as a husband. Asking about the feeding habits of your own children as if they were exotic pets was not the best approach. *What do they normally eat?* The question didn't show a lot of interest in the daily life of my kids, or a general understanding of human biology for that matter. In my defense, I work early in the mornings so I'm not around for the breakfast routine. I assume they eat cereal or yogurt or, I don't know, frittatas.

We had a busy Saturday morning to kick off Daddy Weekend. George had three-year-old karate at nine thirty a.m. for half an hour. Then Lucie had tap dancing a few blocks away at ten thirty. We'll get everybody suited up and whip around the city. I got this.

We wake up, they brush their teeth with diaper cream, everybody pees in the shower, and I put their food and water out in bowls. So far, so good. (Christina doesn't find this funny.)

The first step is to get George in his karate uniform. I desperately want him to wear a headband with a rising sun on it, but he refuses. My ulterior motive for putting him in the class is to eventually have him reenact the final scene of *The Karate Kid* with the other little guys. The headband will make him look like Ralph Macchio, but George doesn't yet appreciate great cinema, so he doesn't get what I'm going for. On a personal note, with some extra outside work with Dad, George *has* learned to execute the crane kick Macchio's Daniel LaRusso used to take down Johnny Lawrence in the All Valley Under 18 Karate Tournament. I feel good about that.

OK, next. Get Lucie into her leotard-and-tights situation. She'll come with us to watch karate and then we'll run over to tap dance. Now where is that leotard? Not in Lucie's dresser. Not in the closet. Not in the washing machine or the dryer. I take another sweep. The clock is ticking now to karate. The sensei does not like tardiness. I ask Lucie where Mom keeps the leotard. She thinks it's in the dresser. It's not. It's not in the dresser. Where else could it be?! Christina, why couldn't you have left it somewhere easy and obvious?! We turn the apartment upside down like cat burglars. As you know, having raised a daughter, Dad, it's the "girl" situations like these where fathers really get themselves in trouble. We have no leotard radar.

At one point Lucie, sensing my simmering frustration, turns to me and says, "Dad, I know how frustrating it can be when you can't find something." Who's the adult here? She's incredible. Where's George, by the way? Playing with the blender? OK, cool.

Finally I call off the search and we call an audible. Lucie will wear the white tights, but with a big black Vanderbilt football T-shirt. It will be the first time her precious Manhattan dance academy has seen SEC football gear. She'll be reppin' the Commodores this morning because, well, we have no choice. Anchor Down, as they say in Nashville. But then Lucie comes out of her room in the giant football shirt and I realize I can't do that to her. Damn.

It's early on a Saturday, but it's New York—there has to be someone who has a leotard. In a scene that now has become iconic in our house, I pick up my iPhone, hit the Siri button, and scream, "LEOTARDS!" Siri tells me she doesn't "understand leotards." I don't either, Siri, but this is no time for chitchat. I try again, louder this time because volume fixes everything: "LEOTARDS!!!" Siri still can't help me. Thanks for nothing, disembodied voice in my phone. Incidentally, if you ever want to make my wife laugh, pick up your iPhone and yell "LEOTARDS!" at it maniacally.

Time to go to Google to find this LEOTARD! Oh, what's the name of that place that has dance clothes and shoes and whatnot? Caprese? No, that's a delicious Italian salad. Spiezio? No, he's a former big league utility infielder. CAPEZIO! That's it! Looks like there's a Capezio we can hit in the twenty minutes we have between karate and tap. It's gonna take some hustle by everybody, but we can do this.

We get George to karate just under the wire. Lucie's wearing the football shirt just in case we can't execute the run to Capezio. George does some respectful bowing, some kicking, some punching, and a lot of looking up at the ceiling along with the other members of his preschool dojo. He gets a piece of red tape on his white belt signifying his, I don't know, attendance, and we're out the door.

The three of us, holding hands, bound through the streets of Manhattan to the Capezio on Amsterdam Avenue. I ask the woman working there to eyeball Lucie and hit me with a size—we don't have time for a *Pretty Woman*-style try-on session here. The Capezio lady nails it! Plus it was like fifteen bucks. I will love Capezio forever for its overall performance in those critical six minutes. Back out the door with five minutes to get up to tap dance class. We're moving again.

As we step into the elevator at the dance studio for the trip up to Lucie's classroom, we exhale. We've pulled it off. Lucie and I high-five. George destroys some Goldfish crackers while still in full karate gear. What I haven't stopped to notice over the past hour or so is the lovely pink messenger bag across Lucie's shoulder. It's where she keeps her tap shoes, she tells me. And other things for tap class.

She reaches in the bag and pulls out her shoes, ready to put them on when we get off the elevator. She peers into the bottom of the bag and says, "Dad! Look!" I don't even have to tell you what was sitting clean and folded in the bottom of the bag. The *tap* bag. Where tap things go. Tap things like leotards. LEOTARDS!!!

Daddy Weekend was off to a tough start, but we

bounced back, and hey, we have a backup leotard now. On Sunday we hit up the Central Park Zoo to visit the penguins and the polar bear. Then we went bowling, where we crushed chicken nuggets and practiced our Pete Weber–style celebrations after taking down even a single pin. We completed a nice trifecta with a trip to Dave & Buster's (aka kids' Vegas). But we didn't go to just any Dave & Buster's—I took them to the one in Times Square. Vast, loud, and packed, it was like the crowded floor of an off-strip casino. A terrifying sea of humanity. The kids had a blast, they won some tickets, and I didn't have to issue any AMBER Alerts, so everybody went home happy. Most importantly, I had run them into the ground. Mission accomplished.

Christina got home that night just moments after we'd done a huge cleanup to create the illusion that everything had gone smoothly all weekend. *How was the weekend, Christina? What? No, we weren't throwing dresser drawers at the wall on Saturday morning looking for an article of clothing you had kindly left right where it belongs.*

Off the full-time kids clock and reintegrating myself into civil society, I got a call from Christina at work the next day saying George had been up vomiting all night. "Was he feeling well yesterday?" she asked. "Any reason he'd be sick?"

Well, I told her, we spent yesterday petting zoo animals in Central Park, eating finger food at a bowling alley, and playing casino games with a thousand tourists from around the world at a Times Square video arcade. Not sure where he picked up the bug. #DaddyWeekend.

"This is not a pony ride"

At the risk of focusing solely on my parental ineptitude and not on my vast Father of the Year credentials, I'll share another moment when Christina wondered briefly about her spousal choice. We were out one afternoon in Montauk, the farthest town east on New York's Long Island. We stopped by Deep Hollow Ranch, which calls itself "the birthplace of the American Cowboy" and "the oldest working ranch in the U.S.A.," established in 1658. A great place where we thought the kids could have some fun.

Lucie and I strode to the front desk to see what Deep Hollow had to offer. Lucie had never been on a horse before, so we were looking for a little walk around the ring to give her an introductory feel for the animal. I said, "My daughter is six and she'd love to go for a ride." The cheery woman behind the counter was happy to oblige and signed Lucie right up. She was given a helmet—guess they have to do that for legal reasons, even just for a slow walk around the stable, I thought. With the help of a stepladder, Lucie happily mounted a horse named J.D. As she settled into the saddle, I noticed most of the group ranged in age from thirty-five to fifty. I inquired again at the desk, where I was told (again?) that Lucie was headed out on a half-hour trail ride. She was saddled up and headed out into cowboy country, without me or anyone else she knew. Let me repeat: She'd never been on a horse. Now she was one step away from dressage.

"Oh, I'm sorry, I misunderstood. She's never been on a horse," I said. Probably not a good idea for her to be out galloping through the trails of Deep Hollow, so I'd better go get her off J.D., huh?

The woman replied, "This is not a pony ride, but she'll be OK." I asked Lucie if she was, in fact, OK going off solo. She had a pretty serious little girl look on her face, but she gave me the thumbs-up. Was she throwing me a signal to come get her? Was she too embarrassed to say she was scared with all those adults around her? I should get her, right? Before I could move in, the guide turned her horse and Lucie—six-year-old Lucie—led the group off on the trail. It was a sweltering summer day, she had no lunch in her stomach, no trip to the potty beforehand, and, did I mention, no experience on a horse. There she went, on a half-hour trail ride at the birthplace of the American Cowboy. A six-year-old in a skirt leading a pack of middle-aged tourists into the unknown.

All this time, Christina had been back at the *actual* pony ride area with George, who rode a horse named Keebler around a little track six times. George insisted, and insists to this day, that the horse was named "Keyboard." We went with "Keyboard."

When Christina and George were finished, they came to check on me and Lucie. It was just me. After a glance at the empty horse ring, Christina's first question naturally was, "Where's Lu?"

"She's out on a little trail ride," I said. "Very little...and brief. Just a walk, really."

"But she doesn't know how to ride a horse. How far are they going?" she wondered.

"Oh, about thirty minutes or so," I said quickly as if there was nothing wrong with the statement.

"What? Wow, I hope she's OK out there by herself," Christina said. What she meant to say was, "You'd better hope she's OK out there by herself." The stakes had been raised.

I needed Lucie to come over that hill at Deep Hollow with a big smile on her face. If she came back in tears, I might lose custody of my children. Come on, Luce. I was willing her courage as I made small talk with the ranch hands and checked my watch. Thirty minutes came and went. Where were they? Oh God, she fell off her horse and the cowboys are tending to her. I imagined J.D. rearing up on his hind legs like the Black Stallion and then running wild up the trail with my daughter clinging for dear life. I had an impulse to jump on one of the horses tied up near us and ride out bareback to get my little girl. I'm only slightly better on a horse than Lucie.

Finally, mercifully, figures on horses began to crest the hill. First the guide. No terror on his face. Good sign. Then, right after him, the cutest little girl you've ever seen, bouncing up and down on ol' J.D., smiling from ear to ear. I must have taken a hundred photographs in a minute. She dismounted and begged to do it again, only next time she wanted the sixty-minute ride, and she wanted the horse to run. Daddy is bailed out by a great kid. Again.

The Principal's Office

I got a text one March morning last year from Christina, telling me that three-year-old George had been sent to the office of the head of school for misbehaving. He and a few buddies had been acting up in Spanish class. I'm not sure I can completely explain why, but as I read the message I got a warm feeling in my chest. For one thing, he'd been kicked out of a *Spanish* class. He was three. Who knows what the little goons had been doing exactly, but I bet the offense was hilarious on its own.

The image of tiny, curly-haired George and his buddies being marched down to see the head of school caused me to smile first, then to laugh out loud at my desk. Did he have any idea he was in trouble? Did he care? How would he answer to the charges? What was he wearing for his hearing? Light-up shoes? The more I pictured him trying to defend himself, the more I laughed. I couldn't wait to get home that night to hear his version of the story—and to try not to laugh as I listened.

I guess you don't know if you're the same kind of father as your own dad until you get there. The laugh I got from George's naughty trip to the principal's office was a pretty good indication. It was an awful lot like the approving laugh you let out, Dad, when I was pelting Duncan with dinner rolls at the Biddy Banquet. Here we go again.

Bill…in His Own Defense

Willie, you've heard me say, time and again, that the day you were born was the happiest day of my life. Unfortunately, your sister heard it too. What I meant, Libby, is that it was my happiest day *to that point*, which is not to say I was happier about her birth either, Son. I'm sure you two will eventually work this out.

In any event, it was exhilarating. You were born on a sunny spring day, May 3, a time when the earth itself is born anew, when young, light-green leaves are sprouting, when dogwoods, cherry trees, and redbuds blossom, and temperatures, even in Chicago, are warming, lifting spirits, sweeping away the gloom. May has always been my favorite month.

I'd said I wanted to have our first baby by my thirtieth birthday, which occurred seven days after you were born.

This portion of our book should be written by your mother, of course, who did by far the most "parenting." Actually, we didn't have "parenting" back then, just parents and kids. Are kids today "childing" their parents?

We didn't have a "parenting style" either ("tiger mom," "helicopter mom," et al). If I had to, I guess I'd probably describe my parenting style as "lucky"—lucky to have a great mother for you and your sister, lucky to be able to have her at home with the two of you, lucky to live on streets where kids could still "just go out and play." Lucky to have two ideal children and lucky to not have stepped on a land mine somewhere along the way to screw that up.

There were different approaches to being parents, of course, from hog-tying to free-range. When you were ten years old and in grade school, a friend of yours rang our doorbell at about ten o'clock one school night and asked if you could walk over to McDonald's, a few blocks away. That was a little too far toward the "hands-off" parenting school for us.

On our block there were parents who shouted—screamed like drill sergeants—at their kids all the time, perhaps because they had too many (five). There were many parents who could never admit their children were the perpetrators of misdeeds and didn't particularly care. Once a child spilled a full glass of red wine on Jody's dress at a dinner party and the child's mother rushed to comfort the little bastard, saying "Oh, honey, are you all right?"

I think your "tough love" approach is brilliant, taking George to precinct headquarters to be reprimanded by a uniformed cop when he doesn't eat his vegetables. And when he does. Bad cop/good cop. I know you recently showed George the jail. New York has some world-class child psychiatrists and I'm sure he'll recover over time.

At his age you were infatuated with fire stations, fire trucks, firefighters and their equipment, including gloves, boots, inhalators, all of it. I was sure that (if you didn't become a pyromaniac) you were going to dedicate your life to firefighting and prevention. Must be something about sons and men in uniform.

We tried to distract you—*Willie! Look over there! An elephant! Keep looking!*—every time we drove by the Central Street fire station. Or we drove circuitous routes to bypass it. Because if you saw the station and we didn't stop, tantrums ensued. You received untold numbers of fire trucks for Christmas and birthdays, remote-control fire trucks, annoying trucks with wailing sirens, ride-on trucks that crashed into tables, their lamps diving off to avoid further danger. There were fire trucks that exploded into a hundred pieces when they hit the wall, requiring a parent to reassemble them ASAP. There were fire trucks that shot real water from their hoses. I'm a little surprised the toy manufacturers didn't include books of matches with the water-squirting trucks for even greater realism.

Sometimes you spotted a fire station before we did and a stop couldn't be avoided. You visited fire stations wherever we went. You were perplexed to see chartreuse fire trucks in Florida, and told that amazing fact to all your friends when you returned home.

You got to know the Central Street firefighters the way George knows cops. They let you wear their heavy hats and sit behind the wheel of a hook-and-ladder. You had your birthday at the Fire Station restaurant. Your mom arranged to have a fire truck come to our block party.

Your favorite show was *Emergency* and you reenacted each episode. Usually the incidents occurred under the dining room table and at all hours. With a fire engine or ambulance in hand you'd awaken us way too early with "Hey, Dad, Mom. Wanna go on a call?"

Jody worked until you were four, something necessary when you're married to a newspaper reporter pulling down twenty grand a year. We both cried when we dropped you off in the morning and sometimes when we picked you up, seeing the assembly line of high chairs occupied by sniffling little baby clients covered in strained foods. The woman who ran this (unlicensed?) operation in her home was a chain-smoker.

We decided together that your mom would stay home with you once your sister was born. Not everyone can manage to do this, but I do believe it was a factor in the two of you turning out so well.

People complain to me of problems they're having with their offspring and ask, sometimes with a note of resentment, "How did your kids turn out so well?"

I mean, Libby didn't even have the Terrible Twos.

Everybody has the Terrible Twos. You, Willie, had not terrible but naughty twos and threes. You did clock another child in day care once. And you had a nasty habit of scooping up shovelfuls of sand at the beach and flinging them on nearby families. After one such sand toss, I shouted at Jody, "We're not raising him right!" Maybe it was time to look into good old-fashioned corporal punishment rather than these silly "time-outs." But we didn't.

We did, however, take stands on certain things. Jody wouldn't allow you to eat sugar cereals. And we wouldn't allow you to have a TV or phone in your bedroom. We didn't have the Internet and cell phones to contend with. If we did, I think we might have had to go full Amish with you.

So you'd go to Tommy's house for a sleepover and load up on Super Sugar Crisp cereal and one of my all-time favorites for sheer audacity: Lucky Charms, which was part cereal, part little colored marshmallows! ("Free Cigarettes Inside!") You'd scarf that down while watching God knows what on the TV in his bedroom.

We braced for those Terrible Teens and they never happened with either of you. Sibling rivalry? Nope. Willie and Libby, four and a half years apart, are the best of friends.

⌒

Learning to parent began pre-birth with reading Dr. Spock's time-honored *Common Sense Book of Baby and Child Care*. We, thankfully, didn't have today's smothering avalanche of books and magazines telling us conflicting ways to do everything—as though this birth thing were a new phenomenon. It makes parents neurotic. Jody ate tuna and soft cheese and had a glass of wine once in a while and you didn't show any ill effects from that, nor from a nasty spill she took water-skiing.

Toward the end of her third term, we took Lamaze classes. We had decided not to have the baby—you!—at home or underwater or anything exotic. Our doctor didn't even own a snorkel.

But Lamaze was somewhat groundbreaking in those days. Both mothers and fathers attended classes, as Lamaze was designed to bring dads into the process and substitute their encouragement for painkillers. Same as back in the Wild West, where they had the patient bite down on a bandanna while they sawed off his foot. What I remember from the classes was that I was to remind your mom to stare at a point on the wall and puff, and to push tennis balls against the small of her back to relieve the agony. OK, if they say so.

I may not have done a good job of all this because when a Lamaze instructor came into what would formerly have been called the "labor room" to cheer us on, Jody shouted at her, "This doesn't work!"

We'd been at home watching *Soul Train* on TV when the contractions (formerly "labor pains") began. When they reached the every-five-minutes mark, I fetched our VW Bug and we drove to Evanston Hospital, where Jody hopped out at the front door, as if she were being dropped off for a hair appointment.

You were born at 8:48 a.m. A nine-pound, five-ounce boy. I was so caught up in things, I hadn't thought to look until a nurse proclaimed, "It's a boy!"

Which brings me to an issue I hesitate to raise at this late date: I'm not sure you're ours. This would explain a lot of your extraordinary attributes. When a nurse brought a baby, which she claimed your mom had just delivered, to your mother's room, I looked at the baby and said, "That's not ours," much as you'd tell a waiter who brings you a pineapple pizza rather than the pepperoni you'd ordered.

The baby I'd seen a few minutes before in the delivery room had scrunched facial features and a purple body. The baby the nurse was holding, post-weighing and -measuring, looked completely different. After careful consideration, we did keep the one she handed us. You. It was like going in to buy a Kia and driving out with a Rolls.

It was my great joy to call both sets of new grandparents and all the new aunts and uncles to deliver the news. (I must say, I did learn in Lamaze to bring a lot of change for the pay phone.)

Is there any better call to make or to receive in your whole life? No. I have been on each end of the line.

I went on a buying frenzy: a box of cigars, flowers, M&M's (a favorite of Jody's), a blue baby outfit, blue balloons, and assorted other blue merchandise. Then I drove to our apartment building to spread the word to our neighbors.

You came home to your own nursery room—yellow, because we hadn't known your gender. In those days most mothers had an initial sonogram to make sure everything was OK, but generally didn't have them again and again, so we didn't know.

Anyway, your nursery had briefly been my den, a manly room painted chocolate brown with some manly brown-and-black striped wallpaper on one wall, a desk, a TV, and an aquarium. I missed it but I don't hold that against you. Anymore.

Jody bathed you in the kitchen sink (moving aside dirty dishes). We pushed you around the neighborhood in a baby carriage. An old-fashioned four-wheeler. A pram.

Back then we didn't put babies in cheap folding strollers (that came later) or those thousand-dollar all-terrain strollers we see today, or backpacks or "front packs" or those precarious-looking slings.

I loved those strolls through the quiet leafy neighborhood. The universe was as it ought to be.

We bought our first house. A few days before we moved in, my father died. You were six months old and a godsend, the only one at his funeral blissfully unaware of the circumstances. You giggled when my brother, David, tossed you around and brought smiles where there were so many tears. Life would go on. My mother, in particular, became bound to you then and there.

My father had been aloof. No hugs. No kisses. No "I love you"s from Dad. These days, of course, everybody hugs everybody. Total strangers, people you've just met, hug you. If you look vaguely familiar, you get a kiss. And people end every phone call with "Love you." Even telemarketers.

Dad was a high school teacher who I think had seen enough kids by the end of the day. He was an amateur photographer and after dinner he would disappear into his basement darkroom and no one was allowed to open the door because light would ruin the film and the prints. He would tune to a radio station that played jazz and swing music from the thirties and forties, which seeped through the door.

I don't think he was pleased with my being not only a mediocre student but a disruptive student, who spent a lot of time sitting in the hall and in after-school detention.

My father did say something that stuck with me. He was a printer, who scrutinized his work with a magnifying glass. "No one ever asks how much time and effort you put into something," he said, "they just see the final result." I think that's why I've never made a deadline, in college, at newspapers, or in television, my entire life.

My "stay-at-home mom," known then as "a mom," attended to our every need: washing, cleaning, ironing, cooking, keeping the books—everything. We didn't have the word *multitasking* yet. She was bright and energetic and these days might well have been a CEO.

Like Jody, my mom did most of the "parenting." My dad was just brought in for major disciplinary procedures, which on a couple of occasions involved chasing, tackling, and shouting, and on one occasion a little ass-whupping.

Our baby boom generation went through a long period of blaming parents—loudly and publicly—for all our problems. I told my mother at her eightieth birthday party that I was a little upset at her for not giving me anything to complain about. I had nothing to talk about when the bitching sessions started.

Some "parenting" comes from outside. I did have a second set of parents, Aunt Janet and Uncle Ed. I worked for eight summers during high school and college at their resort, and whereas my father saw me as a budding juvenile delinquent, Janet and Ed found me to be no less than a comic prodigy. And they were sophisticated; they traveled the world.

They gave me—dare I say it?—self-esteem. Today, of course, it's all about building self-esteem. How do we do it? We give a trophy not only to the first-place team, but also to every member of that team, and indeed to every player in the league for "participation." (OK, in a bike parade on our block Willie did win "Best Decorated Tractor.")

But kids know the score. I was flabbergasted, when we threw away two-thirds of our family possessions to move from a big house to a rather more diminutive New York City apartment, at how easy it was for you to toss out your roomful of trophies, one of which was four feet tall.

Lately there's been quite a push to give girls, in particular, self-esteem through such initiatives as Take Our Daughters to Work Day. There is a sense that our sons already have enough esteem, which of course they don't. I think I shocked another parent sitting next to me at a softball game when I said that instead of taking Libby to work, I was just going to tell Willie he was a worthless bum and that would even things out.

Of course peers do a lot of the parenting too, for better or worse. You hung out with the basketball players, all good students and a few at the top of their class. (Whew!) So getting good grades seemed normal. I do recall you once getting straight A's but for a B-plus in art. Jody went to the school and explained to the art teacher that your lack of artistic ability was a genetic problem and that she herself couldn't draw at all. But the B-plus remained, a permanent blotch on your record. You didn't get that from me. I had average high school grades and took five years to get a BS degree because I was honing my skills playing pinball instead of attending classes. I have to say that by graduation I was a pretty damned good pinball player. But, alas, no pro league.

Now Jody and I are empty nesters living in New York. The thing Jody misses most is you continually bursting through the front door after school, saying, "Hey, Mom, guess what?" And without fail the "what" was something good.

I miss coming home and having you waiting there, wearing your baseball cap and glove and asking, "Hey, Dad! Wanna have a catch?"

⤳ Chapter 16 ⤳

When Bill Became "Bumpa"

BILL

W e bought our new apartment in New York in 2002. It had been the sales model in the building, so we first rid it of perhaps fifteen plastic plants, twelve cheap urns, and several framed pictures of urns. Then your mother spent a great amount of time, effort, and, if I may say so, money, on decor, turning it into a sophisticated adult show-place. Then came the grandchildren.

Newborn Willie and Bill, May 1975

Newborn Lucie and Willie, June 2007

Grandpa Russell Geist and Willie

Grandma Marge and Willie

Grandpa George Lewis and Grandma
Edith "E.E." Lewis with Willie

Grandparents "Jo-Jo" and
"Bumpa" Geist with Lucie
and George

Bill wonders about Lucie and
George sometimes

We felt that rush again, that euphoric rush we recalled from the days you and your sister were born. But this time we were on the receiving end of that blissful call: It was you, Willie, announcing the birth of our first grandchild. A girl. Lucie.

Thank God Christina delivered the baby after rush hour. We grabbed a bottle of champagne and leaped in front of a taxi.

"Are you friggin' nuts?" the driver asked.

"Columbia-Presbyterian Hospital, maternity, fourth floor, and step on it!" I replied.

He drove faster and more recklessly than a stolen van in an LA car chase. Fifteen minutes later we were slapping on our hospital passes and going up to see our—well, their—new baby. With Christina's parents, Vince and Joyce, there along with Christina's siblings, Lucie had already drawn a crowd. Although inconvenient, if Christina had given birth in that stable in Bethlehem we couldn't have been happier.

Jody had waited patiently for this moment to arrive. She'd begun buying and making baby clothes and quilts years before and stashing them away. She'd made a drawing of an addition we were, for some reason, putting on our beach house. The drawing, made a couple of years pre-Lucie, included a mother who looked an awful lot like Christina holding a baby.

About the time Lucie celebrated her first birthday, our apartment decor began to change from "urban adult" to more of a, well, Fisher-Price look. Spilling out from behind the living room furniture, among other places, are great splashes of brightly colored plastic: a farm, a gas station, boxes of Legos, fire engines, police cars, various figurines that the dog eats, you name it.

The decor change accelerated with the arrival of George (named after Grandpa George), our second beloved grandchild, who proclaimed the other day that we have "dozens and dozens"—a word he just learned—of toys. And there are dozens of small design touches to accommodate him, such as the thick gray rubber strip wrapped around the entire edge of the square glass coffee table to prevent at least some of the head wounds that will undoubtedly befall this boisterous boy. When guests inquire about the rubber we explain, "It's a classic reinterpreted design accessory that our interior decorator says is *the* next big thing. You know what they say: 'Accessorize, accessorize accessorize!'"

Decor be damned, I say, when one has grandchildren. The kids need to leave stuff here because they come over so often. They live four blocks away. Libby and her husband, Kevin, have a one-year-old son, Russell, named after my father, but also known to us as the Newborn King. They recently moved from out of state to within a few blocks of us. Skype is one thing, frequent hugging quite another. The kids come over for days or half days and we get hands-on experience.

Lucie, now six, is best described as sweet, beautiful, and talented. She spends much of her time in our apartment at the kitchen table making artful paper bag puppets or illustrating a book she has written. Written!

Also, it was Lucie who gave us our new names. At age one, before they speak words, grandchildren emit unusual sounds when they see grandparents that often become the grandparents' names—permanently. Jody changed her grandparents' names forever from Grandma Elaine to "Gammo" and Grandpa Herb became "Bobby." Willie renamed Grandma Edi "E.E."

Many of Jody's women friends have tried, by repetition, chocolate rewards, but so far nonelectrical means, to train their grandchildren to bestow on them adorable and/or flattering names of the grandparents' choosing. "Coco" is one example. Lucie named Jody "Jo-Jo." I am "Bumpa"—"Bumps," if you know me well. I'm happy with that.

George, four (the last male "Geist" on the family tree), is the more physical of your two and delights in jumping up and down on our bed as if it were a trampoline. When he's doing this, I smack him with a pillow and knock him flat on his back, which makes him laugh. The harder the blow the more he laughs. He gets his licks in too. We look forward to the day when Russie, Libby's toddler, joins the fight.

They like it at Jo-Jo and Bumpa's house. We keep large, survivalist-size supplies of Popsicles, ice-cream bars, and lollipops on hand. Let's not have a conversation about that.

Grandparenting *is* better than parenting. You love your kids and grandkids just the same but it's like having two full-time nannies: You can hand grandkids back whenever they're tired or fussy or screaming or crying or smelly: "Awww, the baby wants his mommy."

We're learning the rule changes that have been implemented since you were a child, such as avoiding peanut butter, the diet staple of generations of Americans; putting babies to sleep on their backs, which they used to say would definitely cause them to choke; and keeping kids buckled into car seats in the back until they reach the size of black bears.

Although the rules have changed, your sense of humor about your kids seems familiar. We love getting the "quote of the day" e-mails from you and Christina, such as:

> Visiting friends at their beach club George was heard counting one, two, three (unintelligible) as he jumped off the diving board. Several jumps later we asked him what he was saying and he said, "One, two, three, sauvignon blanc." He explained, saying this is what Mommy says every day!

Or:

> Lucie getting ready for her first day of kindergarten took her own shower and then Christina offered to blow-dry her hair with a "Hello, gorgeous" hairdo. "It's important to look your best on the first day," Christina offered. Lu answered, "I know, that's why I put-ed on lipstick and makeup!"

The biggest difference in our child-rearing is that you're raising city kids, who are much more sophisticated than you were at four and six (no offense) and have had a lifetime of rich experiences already. We love our tradition of taking Lucie to a Broadway musical every year, even though she has to hold her ears every time Captain Hook or Miss Hannigan is onstage.

They're comfortable riding the subway, accompanied,

and know to get on the M104 bus to get to school. Imagine our surprise when five-year-old Lucie stuck out her hand to hail a taxi! They both casually greet our doormen, "Good morning, Felix," just as Eloise would, and they giggle when Jose sings them the Elmo song in a perfect Elmo voice.

George asks a lot of questions. Tough ones at times. We were sitting on the couch the other day when he asked, "Bumpa, what is Heaven?" I'm no religious scholar, but I tried to answer as best I could. Unfortunately, he had follow-up questions (Where? Who goes there? Why? Are there toys in heaven?). It turned into a whole…conversation.

If you'd asked me that question thirty-some years ago I probably would have said, "It's a place made of ice-cream bars. Want one, Willie?"

Epilogue

Well, Dad, that conversation with four-year-old George about Heaven is officially deeper than any you and I have ever had. Maybe I've just been asking the wrong questions. My pre-K son skipped straight to the Afterlife. Impressive.

The great gift of writing this book (besides the opportunity to teach you over the phone how to attach a Word document to an e-mail) is that it allowed us to sit down and review our life together. Not many people get that chance. It got us talking about thirty-nine years of nearly uninterrupted laughter. It also got you to put down on paper your memories about a war you'd locked away, and to look in the eye a disease you've fought so hard to ignore.

This printed-and-bound trip through our history took me back to the bus stop along Route 17 in Ridgewood, New Jersey, where a young boy, his mother, and his baby sister waited excitedly to pick you up when you came home from your big new job at the *New York Times*.

The book reminded me that we spent nights in those days talking in baseball announcers' voices, placing our neighbors in a ridiculous starting lineup: "Batting cleanup and doing the catching tonight...Claire Witz! Dagmar Randolph's over at third...swingin' a hot bat right now."

I got to think about all the times over the years you borrowed your uncle Ed's famous line, "I could care less!" accompanied by the swirling of Scotch and ice around a glass. Yes, we know it's "I *couldn't* care less," but you always stayed true to the original. Your use of that phrase, spoken in Ed's voice, meant you were doing something that made us feel like big shots—ordering room service or upgrading the rental car. *"Aw, hell, I could care less!"*

I got to laugh again about the time those nice ladies ahead of us on the first tee stopped to tell you how much they loved you and your work. As they putted a few minutes later, we teed off. In an uncharacteristic display of distance and accuracy, you drove the green and drilled one of your admirers. She turned around, yelled something terrible at you, and flipped you off. A quick change of heart.

I laughed thinking about the time I handed you your beautiful infant granddaughter, Lucie, round and still without hair, and you said, "You know, she looks a lot like Khrushchev." I think I was supposed to be offended, but she really was a dead ringer for the stout Soviet leader.

Writing this book allowed me to catalogue your brave and ongoing protests against small signs of progress. You fought a lonely battle against mandatory seat belts, defending your right to go through the windshield while passive-aggressively taking several minutes to find the belt and pull it across your body while the rest of us waited. You continue your jihad against watered-down skim milk—"Why

don't I just go drink from the garden hose. Same thing."
You always, without fail, tear the potato chip bag the wrong
way—up the side—eliminating any possibility of resealing
it and ensuring the chips go stale. You reject on principle
organic food and veganism. I can't remember which principle that is, but you stand firm on it. You reject studies sug-
gesting yet another food that will kill us (contending that
the next study will suggest the opposite). And you have no
time for today's obsessive hand-washing. Wait, I just realized you're George Carlin.

But I also remembered as I went along that you used
to write notes of encouragement and leave them for me.
Some of them were a full handwritten page—about school,
about basketball…about life. Others were short messages
of pride and love scribbled on the offertory card in church.
Those were our conversations.

When I tuck Lucie in at night, she often asks, "Daddy,
tell me a story about when you were a little boy." Well,
Luce, this is it. The story of me and my dad.

Acknowledgments

There is plenty of blame to go around for this father-son collaboration. You could begin with our longtime shared literary agent and friend Tom Connor, who planted the seed for the book and stood by as we recklessly poured our lives onto the page. Thank you for the inspiration, Tom. We think.

Our wonderful editor Gretchen Young laughed at our family stories over lunch one day and convinced us that book-buying readers might do the same. Gretchen patiently edited and organized generations of messy Geist history into a coherent book, with the help of her assistant Allyson Rudolph. You're lucky as a writer if you find an editor who gets you. Gretchen always has. She is the best.

Our big thanks to Jamie Raab, Deb Futter, Emi Battaglia, Jimmy Franco, Rick Wolff, Andrew Duncan, Rick Cobban, Diane Luger, and the entire production team at Grand Central for their support from our first meeting forward. Now, remember in our pitch when we guaranteed we'd outsell your superstar million-selling authors? We never put that in writing, did we? If so, we should talk offline.

Love to Jody, mother nonpareil and the better half—make that better three-fourths—of this parental couple, who lived through all this and more. She and Christina are the real stars of this book, and of our lives. They were with us every step of the way, writing, editing, laughing, crying, and filling in the blanks. In exchange for a lifetime of love, they each will receive one (1) free well drink at the book party.

Our big love to daughter and sister, Libby, who's been at the center of just about everything in this book. Smart, funny, beautiful, and talented, she is by far the most impressive Geist.

And we are forever beholden to the extended Geist and Lewis families for providing us such a wealth of material. For those of you who will face prosecution at either the state or federal level as a result of what is published here, stay strong in prison. We'll visit when we can.

Young Willie's Father's Day drawing for Bill. He nailed the hair.